SURVIVAL AND DISEMBODIED EXISTENCE

STUDIES IN
PHILOSOPHICAL PSYCHOLOGY

Edited by
R. F. HOLLAND

SURVIVAL AND
DISEMBODIED EXISTENCE

by

TERENCE PENELHUM

LONDON
ROUTLEDGE & KEGAN PAUL
NEW YORK : HUMANITIES PRESS

First published 1970
by Routledge & Kegan Paul Ltd
Broadway House, 68–74 Carter Lane
London, E.C.4
Printed in Great Britain by
W & J Mackay & Co Ltd, Chatham
© *Terence Penelhum*
ISBN 0 7100 6723 2

CONTENTS

CONTENTS

To Edith

ACKNOWLEDGMENTS

SOME of the material in Chapters 7, 8 and 9 appeared in a paper in Volume I of the Proceedings of the Seventh Inter-American Congress of Philosophy, Les Presses de l'Université Laval, Quebec, 1967, pages 353–69. I am grateful to the Press for their kind permission to include it.

Among the many philosophers whose discussions and criticisms have helped me formulate the arguments in this essay I would particularly like to express gratitude to those who participated in a seminar on this subject at the University of Washington Summer Institute, 1968, especially Messrs. Keyt, Melzack, Richman, Siegler and Saslaw. Without them the arguments of Chapters 2 and 3 would be even more dubious than they are. No one who writes about Personal Identity at the present time can fail to acknowledge the original and perceptive contributions of Sydney Shoemaker, whose work originally stimulated much of my own thinking on this topic, some of which appears in what follows. I have also learned a great deal on this subject from my colleague J. J. MacIntosh.

CHAPTER 1

PRELIMINARIES

THE objective of this study is to examine some of the logical problems connected with the belief that all, or some, persons survive death. I shall not attempt to evaluate the quality of the empirical evidence which is said to support this belief. Nor shall I attempt to evaluate any one of the many religious doctrines with which this belief is usually associated. To some readers, most particularly those who are committed to some doctrinal scheme of which the belief in survival forms a part, or for whom such a scheme is at least an open option, the question of whether the logical problems this belief raises are intractable ones is a question of real personal concern. To others, who may have rejected all such doctrinal schemes on other grounds, the question will have a largely clinical interest, since even if these logical problems do not prove intractable, the belief in survival will still be rejected as false, even though it proves not to be incoherent. Of course, to either group a discussion of the notion of survival can have independent philosophical value as a means of clarifying our everyday notions of human personality, for one is bound to feel one understands this better after confronting the question of whether or not it could continue to exist after death. But whatever the nature of any philosopher's concern with it, it is one philosophical question of which the topicality outside the confines of the profession hardly needs stating; for it is obvious that a doctrine of survival in some form has been extremely widespread throughout human history and has formed a critically important part of many religious traditions.

In so far as I shall make reference to any religious tradition at all, it will be to the Western Christian tradition. I do in fact hope that what I shall say will have bearing upon those beliefs about human survival of death which are part of it. On the other hand, my procedure will be to investigate two major possible versions of the belief that persons survive death, and leave it to others to decide how far these two versions coincide with Christian teachings about these matters. This seems the only way to provide in a short space for reasonable clarity of definition of the notions to be examined. The belief in survival has clearly taken more than one form as the Christian tradition has grown and changed, and I do in fact think that the perplexities connected with the versions I shall discuss bear closely upon the intelligibility of the forms it has taken; but apart from a few immediate comments I shall not attempt to argue that they do have this bearing, once I have begun considering them.

The two major forms of the belief in survival that I shall discuss are (a) the belief in disembodied survival, and (b) the belief in bodily resurrection. The term 'disembodied' suggests of course that a being alleged to exist in this fashion had a body before death but now does not. To some extent this restriction is an artificial one, since many of the questions about disembodied survival are of the form: how could a being with no body possess such-and-such a property or exercise such-and-such a skill? And questions of this form bear on the general issue of the conceivability of *incorporeal* personal existence, which might very well include the existence of personal beings who not only do not or will not have bodies, but never have had. While this wider application will be possible, and I shall in fact once or twice stress it incidentally,[1] I shall keep to the language of *dis*embodiment for the following reasons: (i) it is the question of whether corporeal human beings will survive their physical death that primarily concerns those who reflect on these issues; (ii) the problem of the identity of the post-mortem person with the pre-mortem person turns very largely upon the continuance or non-continuance of the body, or at least seems to do so; (iii) it might turn out that certain properties or skills can be ascribed without logical difficulties to a bodiless being only if one can evade the question of how such a being could come to *acquire* them without a body: an issue which can be evaded by the suggestion that they might have been acquired during the pre-mortem bodily state and retained.

The phrase 'bodily resurrection' suggests that the person survives in the same body that he or she had in the pre-mortem life, even if the period between death and resurrection is considerable. The more orthodox reading of the traditional doctrine of resurrection does seem to imply this claim of the miraculous raising of the person's original body. (An unreflective adherence to this was the major source of opposition

[1] See Chapter 10.

to cremation or the medical dissection of corpses.) On the other hand, the doctrine can be, and has been, held in a form which implies that the person is indeed re-created in a body, but that that body is not numerically identical with the one which the person had in the pre-mortem life. It is easy to see that any very radical emphasis on the *transformation* which the body under-goes in resurrection is likely to blur the distinction between these two versions. It is almost as easy to see also that if the dissolution of the pre-mortem body prior to resurrection is assumed, the distinction between the two versions runs the risk of becoming merely verbal, since it is arguable that even if some-one says we can look forward to the first situation, we *can* only have the second. While this particular ambiguity will in fact resolve itself, I shall proceed on the assumption that it is the former doctrine that we are examining, unless I state otherwise. It is, incidentally, this doctrine that seems the more natural interpretation of St Paul in I Corinthians and of the Apostles' Creed.

The belief in disembodied survival and the belief in bodily resurrection can, of course, be combined. They are combined if someone believes that there is a gap in time between death and resurrection, and that during that period the person survives without any body. But although they can be combined, they clearly do not necessarily have to be. Not only is it possible to believe in disembodied survival without believing in bodily resurrection, but it is also possible to believe in bodily resurrection without believing in disembodied survival, viz. by asserting that the person has no form of life whatever between death and resurrection, that nothing continues during the gap. It is also possible to hold that resurrection is instantaneous, and that there is no time-gap at all. This somewhat more complex view I shall examine separately at a later point. The possibilities of combination and separation, and the extent to which the two doctrines can be, or are, independent of one another, are matters of critical importance.

I shall not discuss other possible versions of the belief in survival. I shall ignore the doctrine of metempsychosis. I shall ignore, for different reasons, palliative doctrines which proclaim that people 'survive' in the memories of others, or in their achievements, or in the progress of the race or family. I shall ignore the belief that some psychical remnant of the person is absorbed into a collective world-soul. And I shall not discuss belief in ghosts or shades. On the other hand, while I am not directly concerned with it, I shall not be able altogether to avoid discussion of the concept of reincarnation. One possible version of the belief in reincarnation is presumably the belief that someone now existing is identical with some person who died before his birth. This is sometimes held together with the belief that the person now existing carries, as marks of his previous existence, memories of his former life; though this is not always added. If it is added, however, the resulting doctrine, however clear or obscure we may feel it to be, has many points of similarity to the doctrine of bodily resurrection, especially in that version which suggests the resurrection-body and the pre-mortem body are not numerically identical. It is because of this similarity that the possibility of reincarnation has sometimes exercised those philosophers who have discussed those aspects of the problem of personal identity that bear most directly on the problem of the possibility of survival. Consequently some incidental discussion of the concept of reincarnation will form part of my argument, but not for its own intrinsic interest.

While I shall not argue that the versions of the belief in survival that I consider are in fact the same as those which Christianity has proclaimed, it does seem clear that some doctrine of survival is a logically necessary part of it, so that the conceptual difficulties the notion gives rise to cannot be dismissed lightly by apologists. Recent philosophical discussions suggest at least two reasons for this opinion. (i) Flew and others have said that religious discourse fails to contain genuine assertions because nothing is allowed by those who engage in it to count as a possible falsification of their apparent assertions about God and his relationship to the world.[1] It seems inadequate to reply here that such criticism is just an archaic application of the Verification Principle, for the terms used by believers to speak of God are usually familiar ones, learned originally in their application to human beings, in contexts where statements containing them are subject to verification and falsification procedures. To insist that such procedures are not apposite when these terms figure in religious assertions is to leave them without clear patterns of use. John Hick[2] has attempted to answer this problem by arguing that the verification of religious beliefs is indeed available, but is eschatological. I incline to the view that only some such move as this enables the apologist to hold that Christian

---

[1] See the 'Theology and Falsification' debate.
[2] In 'Theology and Verification'.

beliefs do have a verification-structure.[1] If this is true, the logical possibility of survival of death becomes central to any possible answer to these sceptical attacks. (ii) It is hard to see how the traditional perplexities of the Problem of Evil admit of an answer without the possibility of reference to the after-life. If one assumes that the primary obstacle to the reconciliation of the belief in an all-powerful and all-good deity with the recognition of the existence of evil is the difficulty of holding that no suffering is pointless, then the apologist is forced to look outside the sphere of mortal life for the possibility of recompense for innocent sufferers, or for the chance of exercise of those qualities of soul which our status as free agents is said to enable us to develop through the sufferings that confront us.

Although I have excluded it from my main purview, it would be unfortunate not to mention one recent discussion as to which possible version of the belief in survival is the authentic Christian one. No doubt many people who consider themselves to hold Christian doctrines *say* they believe in the doctrine of disembodied survival—or, as they would no doubt express it, the doctrine of the immortality of the soul. Many of them would combine this with an apparent belief in an afterworld that has spatial characteristics, with no clear consciousness of the obvious dangers of inconsistency. Oscar Cullmann has recently argued[2] that the *primitive* Christian belief is that of the resurrection of the body. This hope he contrasts with the

---

[1] I argue this in a forthcoming general work on philosophy of religion to be published by Random House.

[2] In *Immortality of the Soul or Resurrection of the Dead?*

Platonic doctrine of the immortality of the soul. He compares the serenity of Socrates in the *Phaedo*, viewing his approaching death as the liberation of the soul from the alien bondage of the material body, with the fear and horror experienced by Jesus, for whom death is the great destroyer and ultimate enemy, that can only be defeated if God miraculously intervenes and re-creates what death has destroyed. To Socrates, he says, the person, identified with the soul, continues through and after death, whereas to Jesus the person, thought of as soul and body together, is destroyed by death and only lives after it if God reverses this destruction. The primitive Christian expectation is, he says, that of the re-creation of the embodied person. H. A. Wolfson has replied[1] that these contrasting attitudes of Socrates and Jesus can both be reconciled with the expectation that the soul will continue in existence after death: the differing attitudes could be regarded as different responses to the fact of the *separation* of the soul from the body. He claims that although the doctrine of bodily resurrection *is* Christian and not Greek, it is not held instead of, but in combination with, the belief in the independent existence of the soul after death; the Christian claim is merely that at a later time the soul will *rejoin* the body it has left. He argues impressively that it is this combined doctrine that is held by the majority of the Fathers. I cannot enter this argument, but have one comment. Whether the early Christians believed in disembodied survival as well as resurrection or not, it is clear that their eschatological expectations were

[1] 'Immortality and Resurrection in the Philosophy of the Church Fathers.'

tied to the doctrine of resurrection: that the person who has to stand for a man's misdeeds at the last is the resurrected, whole person. This would seem to make the question of the addition of an interim period of disembodied existence one of minor importance for an understanding of the Christian attitudes to death. But it is in any case always of value in theology to ask what is essential to a doctrine and what is not. If it were agreed that the doctrine of resurrection is the distinctively Christian contribution to human thought about survival, then it would be of great value to decide how far this doctrine can stand alone; particularly if, as I shall hold, there are far greater logical difficulties in the concept of disembodied survival than in that of bodily resurrection. For whatever distinct elements a religious tradition may contain, one element may be more readily expendable in the face of philosophical criticism than another.

Our problem, then, is to assess the intelligibility of these two alternative concepts of survival of death. This may seem very odd. For we are not here encountering some metaphysical doctrine that has been constructed by one group of philosophical specialists and is being questioned by another. We are talking of a doctrine close at least to one held to by millions, and thoroughly familiar. The strangeness of suggesting that it is unintelligible (rather than intelligible but false) should be emphasized. We might here bear in mind Butler's famous remark that 'Whether we are to live in a future state, as it is the most important question which can possibly be asked, so it is the most intelligible one which can be expressed in language'.[1]

[1] 'Of Personal Identity.'

The very existence of enquiries like the present one counts against the truth of Butler's assertion, but the force of what he says does make it necessary to distinguish between one charge of senselessness and another. I propose in what follows to say that I can attach no sense to some expression when I am unable to understand what it means. This comment will, in other words, be merely autobiographical, though I hope that when I make it, it will not turn out to be the case that I am at a unique disadvantage. I propose to say that a belief is unintelligible if it can be shown to be incoherent in some way. This might come about if the belief contains concealed contradictions. It might come about if the belief can only be expressed by the use of notions that its adherents have said they have discarded. It might come about if it can only be expressed by the use of notions which, though not overtly discarded, are logically ruled out by restrictions that *have* overtly been made. The unintelligibility of some belief has to be shown by argument; and the claim that some belief is unintelligible is, therefore, a claim to some philosophical achievement, whereas the statement that I cannot attach sense to it is not. I do not suggest that these two expressions exhaust the range of difficulties of understanding. I would not use either expression to describe someone's belief in round squares or married bachelors. The failure of such beliefs is too *obvious* for them to fit the category of the unintelligible; and the very fact that we can see at once that they contain contradictions indicates that we can attach sense to the expressions used to state them. The area of religious beliefs is full of doctrines to which multitudes seem able to attach sense, but which philosophers are apt to say are unintelligible. The belief in survival is one of the most notorious of these.

There are two main areas of difficulty which philosophers have concentrated upon. In the first place, they have wondered whether the sort of existence envisaged after death can be intelligibly described: whether, that is to say, a sufficient number of the predicates that we would feel it necessary to ascribe to a being before it could be called a person at all can in fact be ascribed to a being that no longer has a body, or who has a resurrected body. In the second place, they have wondered whether the sort of being whose existence is predicted, even if properly called a person, can be identified with any particular pre-mortem person. If the post-mortem person is not identifiable with Jones, then its future existence is merely an interesting natural (or supernatural) fact, but not of personal moment to Jones or Jones's relatives and friends. In predicting the future existence of such a being after his own death, Jones is not predicting *his own* future existence. And only if he can predict his own future existence can he be entitled to *anticipate* it, either with pleasure or with fear.

These two problems cannot be wholly separated. In particular it is not possible to enquire into the possibility of ascribing predicates to a post-mortem being without at some stage raising the issue of the criteria of identity of the post-mortem being through time in the post-mortem state—an issue which would clearly bear upon the possibility of such a being being identical with a pre-mortem person. For predicates are ascribed to subjects, and the self-identity of the subject is a precondition of applying to it any predicates whose ascription implies some lapse of time. But in order to avoid ignoring, or exaggerating, one set of logical difficulties because of its connection with another, I shall impose an admittedly artificial division on the discussion that follows. I shall begin by discussing the question of what predicates can be properly ascribed to post-mortem beings, without questioning whether the qualities and activities attributed to them can really be said to belong to a continuing identical subject. This will make it possible to consider what kind of life and activity we are equipped to consider post-mortem beings to enjoy, as distinct from the kind of life and activity sometimes thought to be available to them. I shall then turn to the question that has been put aside previously, and examine the problem of the identity of post-mortem beings, both with regard to their persistence as individuals through time in the post-mortem state, and with regard to the possibility of regarding them as identical with pre-mortem beings like ourselves.

It is possible to prune the discussion at the outset. It is obvious that the doctrine of disembodied survival raises more problems in both categories than the doctrine of resurrection. If resurrected persons have bodies like ours, there seems no great difficulty in understanding the ascription to them of most of the predicates we ascribe to ourselves. Nor does there seem to be any obvious difficulty in understanding how they can retain their personal identity in the future state. These questions only become seriously difficult if the proponent of the doctrine of resurrection puts inordinate weight upon the extent to which the resurrected person exists in a *transformed* state radically unlike this present one. The greater the transformation, the greater the difficulty of understanding the description of this state. Failing any detailed account of it, we cannot investigate how great the emphasis on its transformedness needs to be; and I shall proceed, *faute de mieux*, as though the future state can appropriately be conceived as sufficiently like the present one for the bulk of our everyday notions to apply to it. The major difficulty that this still leaves is the difficulty of identifying with *us* the persons that it is alleged will exist in this state, so that we can anticipate *being them*. But with the doctrine of disembodied survival problems of enormous complexity arise at every turn. One can wonder whether the predicates we ascribe to pre-mortem persons can apply to beings without bodies. One can wonder whether beings without bodies can intelligibly be said to remain identical through time in their disembodied state. And one can wonder whether they can be identified with pre-mortem, embodied, persons. I shall therefore confine the discussion of post-mortem predication and post-mortem identity through time to the case of disembodied survival; but the question of the identity of pre-mortem and post-mortem beings will embrace both doctrines.

It is obviously necessary, while discussing the identity of post-mortem and pre-mortem persons, to lean on recent arguments of a more general kind concerning the criteria of personal identity. While I shall make use of these only in so far as our central theme requires this, the fact that it has always been a matter of philosophical controversy what the criteria of pre-mortem personal identity are shows that it will be impossible to consider the possibility of post-mortem persons being identical with former pre-mortem ones without taking sides in this controversy. There have been two main competing views. One is that the criterion for the re-identification of a person through time is the identity of the body which he has, i.e. that it is a necessary or a sufficient condition of saying that a person now before us is Jones that the body of this person is the body that Jones had. The other is that the criterion for the re-identification of a person through time is the set of memories he has, i.e. that it is a necessary or a sufficient condition of saying that the person now before us is Jones that he should have memories of doing actions that Jones did or of thinking thoughts that Jones thought, or of undergoing experiences that Jones underwent. The literature of personal identity is very largely concerned with how far if at all each of these standards is indeed necessary or sufficient, and how they are related to each other. Clearly the doctrine of disembodied survival depends on the view that the bodily criterion of identity is not fundamental, or is at least expendable. If the identity of a person is necessarily connected with the persistence of his body through time, then it is logically impossible for a person to survive the death of his body. If, on the other hand, there is no such necessary connection, it is at least logically possible that death is not the end of a person but merely one very major event in his history. Further, if the necessary connection is not between bodily identity and personal identity but between personal identity and memory, then it might be that a disembodied person might be said to be the same as some pre-mortem person because he might remember events and actions in his previous existence. It is surely this consequence that has always lent special interest to the otherwise merely intriguing *puzzle-cases*. These are stories, usually (though not always) invented by philosophers, whose very easy intelligibility seems to suggest that the memory-criterion of personal identity is the more fundamental of the two. Two such examples are found, briefly stated, in Locke, who is the classical source of attempts to define self-identity in terms of memory:

(i) Should the soul of a prince, carrying with it the consciousness of the prince's past life, enter and inform the body of a cobbler, as soon as deserted by his own soul, everyone sees he would be the same *person* with the prince, accountable only for the prince's actions.[1]

(ii) Had I the same consciousness that I saw the ark and Noah's flood, as that I saw an overflowing of the Thames last winter, I could no more doubt that I who write this now, that saw the Thames overflowed last winter, and that viewed the flood at the general deluge, was the same *self* . . . than that I who write this am the same *myself* now whilst I write . . . that I was yesterday.[2]

Locke's confidence in the import of these exercises of imagination is so great that there is little attempt to separate the story from its interpretation; and the confidence, which has not been shared by all readers,[3]

[1] Locke, *Essay on Human Understanding*, Book II, Chapter 27, Section 15.

[2] Locke, *op. cit.*, Section 16.

[3] See Flew, 'Locke and the Problem of Personal Identity'.

I shall try to show later to be unfounded. The two cases do seem to be intelligible enough, however. Case (i) is that of a circumstance in which someone seems to have come to have the body that until recently belonged to a contemporary. Case (ii) is that of a circumstance in which someone seems to remember seeing, and therefore to have been present at, events that took place many years before the birth of his present body. Let us call (i) a case of *putative bodily transfer*, and call (ii) a case of *putative reincarnation*. A recent actual case of the second sort (one, that is, in which a claim of reincarnation has actually been made) is that of 'Bridey Murphy'.[1] A more recent imaginary case of the first sort is supplied by A. M. Quinton in his essay 'The Soul'.[2] He asks us to imagine two men, B and C, the first of whom is 'a dark, tall, thin puritanical Scotsman' and the other 'a fair, short, plump apolaustic Pole', with each of whom I have engaged in activities suited to their temperaments; then to imagine one day the tall thin man requesting me to continue with him the activities previously pursued with C, which he claims as his own, rather than those of B, which he does not appear to recall and which he disowns, and the short plump man making similar requests to me to continue with him B's activities, which he now claims as his own, etc. He argues that we should rather say that B and C had switched bodies than that they had switched characters and memories. Those who invent cases of this sort claim that it is possible to construct imaginary

[1] M. Bernstein, 'The Search for Bridey Murphy'. This case is defended by C. J. Ducasse in Chapter XXV of *The Belief in a Life After Death*.

[2] A. M. Quinton, 'The Soul'.

situations in which we would be correct in saying that the identity of some particular person had transcended that of some particular body. For the doctrine of disembodied survival to be possible, of course, more than this is needed. It is necessary to be able to say, much more radically, that personal identity might continue with no body at all. If the former is inadmissible, the latter is also; but the admissibility of the former thesis does not entail that of the latter, though it might seem to open the way to it. We must therefore see whether the puzzle cases do, in fact, have the implications their inventors claim, and whether admitting these does anything to further the case for personal disembodiment. It would be surprising if the results of this did not bear also on the identity of resurrected persons.

A brief comment, finally, on Psychical Research. Just as the amateurish imaginative exercises of philosophers yield us examples that are intended to force us to admit the intelligibility of certain forms of speech, so the literature of Psychical Research contains many examples, some at least recorded and documented with great objectivity and skill, which it is very natural indeed to account for in terms of the survival of formerly known persons. Some of the most striking of these are apparent mediumistic communications. I shall not attempt an assessment of any of these. In a clear sense the logical investigation of the concept of survival is prior to such an assessment, since only if the concept of survival is coherent can it be offered as an explanation of these, or any, examples. On the other hand, anyone who argues that the doctrine of survival is unintelligible is ruling out, *a priori*, the most natural account of these phenomena, and the one in terms of which those involved in them present them. This should not be done lightly, since if this explanatory recourse is ruled out, we may find ourselves resorting to theses of equal or greater obscurity, or refusing, like ostriches, to scrutinize the evidence at all. But the fact that the doctrine of survival should not be dismissed lightly is obvious enough for quite other reasons.

CHAPTER 2

DISEMBODIED EXISTENCE AND PERCEPTION

WHATEVER the historical reasons may be, large numbers of those who believe that men survive their deaths *think*, at least, that they believe that they survive without a body. Many of those who think they believe this also seem to believe things that are not obviously consistent with it—for example, that some of those who survive thus are able to forgather in groups to play musical instruments. It is not of philosophical interest to explore very patent inconsistencies. What is of value is to see how far such inconsistencies can be avoided if the doctrine of disembodied survival is stated with care. Some philosophers have argued, without very extensive examination, that the doctrine is always beset, even at a more subtle level, with this kind of contradiction.

There is only one way to deal with a criticism of this sort: to take a particular predicate, selected because it is one of that large number that one would feel it necessary to be able to ascribe to any being said to be a person, and decide whether any being to which that predicate can be applied must, in logic, be one with a body; then to take another such predicate, and ask the same thing about it. After this has been done in a large number of cases, one must tot up the number that do (with appropriate disclaimers) still seem usable, and those that (even with disclaimers) do not, and make a judgment: whether a being to which only those in the first list apply would properly be called a person at all. Such a judgment, which runs a clear risk of being inconclusive, has to be positive for it to be true that we have (or can construct) a concept of disembodied personal existence that has sufficient content to be employed in coherent predictions.

This procedure is unsatisfying to those who wish for the conclusiveness that derives from generality. They are more likely to be satisfied by considerations about the identity of disembodied beings that have, for the present, been put aside. I shall at this stage make an assumption that I shall subsequently criticize, that we can form a sufficiently clear idea of what it would be for a disembodied person to persist through time, or be identifiable with a pre-mortem person. But I shall also put aside certain general epistemological considerations that I shall not investigate at all, even though their bearing is obvious. It is often pointed out that disembodied persons would be imperceptible, so that it might well be impossible, even if there are any of them, for us to be aware of their presence, and might indeed be impossible for any one of them to be aware of the presence of the others. Let us suppose this is true. It would show, probably, that we would never be in a position to make a true statement about the present state of any disembodied being using any of the predicates we are considering. Would this in turn show that the claim that there is, *now*, a disembodied being that is in some state normally described by the use of one such predicate, is an unintelligible claim? Perhaps it would; but only if we leaned on some principle according to which one can only understand a statement, even if it contains familiar words, if one knows how one would discover whether it is true. Principles that yield this result are readily to hand. But the plausibility of any one of them is no greater than that of the flat assertion that any particular statement ruled out by it is unintelligible. Even if this were not so, the plausibility of the principle would certainly be affected by any decisions that we could come to independently regarding statements that would be ruled out by it. I therefore make the methodological presumption that it might be possible to make and to understand statements about disembodied persons even though we would not be in a position to specify a way of ascertaining their truth, and consider only problems that still remain if this assumption is made. There are many of these, and making this presumption will enable us to examine them.

Even with these provisos, our problem needs further definition. (i) The problem of predication as I have stated it is one of *attenuation*. In saying that a postmortem person has no body, one says that a great many predicates we ascribe to persons can be ascribed no longer, and the decision that faces us is a decision whether enough still *can* be applied. A disembodied person cannot walk, smile, frown, sleep, or turn his head. Perhaps, though, he might perceive, imagine, form intentions, or feel angry; though in all these cases many normal implications would no longer be attached. What, however, of the fact that those who anticipate disembodied personal existence would expect to be able in that state to do or experience many things of which we have no conception here and now, in *addition* to those of which we do? The only response to this claim is to point out that although the passage from embodied to disembodied existence might very well involve an addition of new powers and experiences as well as a subtraction of old ones, the passage here and now from the *concept* of embodied personal existence to the *concept* of disembodied personal existence involves a process of subtraction almost exclusively. For any powers or experiences that are added have to be describable to us here and now for them to form any part of the content of the concept whose intelligibility we are examining. And only if that concept has a minimal content can we formulate a prediction whose truth or falsity can be evaluated. Mystery, though natural and expected, cannot be complete.

(ii) To say that a particular predicate P can be intelligibly applied to a disembodied person is not, it must be emphasized, to claim that it could be *learned* by a person in a disembodied state. It is only to claim that intelligible statements containing it could be made *about* him. Making use of our methodological presumptions, we can say that if he can make statements about himself (and *to* himself) this might be because he inherits from the pre-mortem state the necessary understanding of what the predicate P means.

(iii) It is essential, further, to distinguish between the question, 'Can we say of him that predicate P applies?' (a question which will presuppose some story about his situation which he might or might not be in a position himself to know to be true), and the question, 'Could he, even inheriting the language that contains P, apply it correctly to himself?' If the answer to this second question is regularly in the negative, this might prompt a third question, 'Could a disembodied person come to give P a *new use*, corresponding in some respects but not all to its old use?' It is important to remember that our being able to say of him that he can do or experience something does not entail his awareness that he can do it or experience it; nor does his being satisfied that he can do it or experience it entail that he in fact can.

(iv) Finally, we might find that the intelligible application of P to a disembodied person is called into question when we reflect on the obvious liabilities of disembodiment, but not *decisively*; so that it would only be *clear* that a disembodied person could have P applied if we were prepared to ascribe to him either some occult new power or the occult extension of some power that is already familiar in a more modest form. It is valuable to see how far the retention of an ability is logically compatible with the subtraction of the body and how far it would also require the addition of some extraordinary mental power.

Given the necessity of severe selection, I shall discuss two groups of predicates that are frequently used to talk of persons, and that seem to have some *prima facie* claim to be applicable to disembodied ones. I shall take first a group of predicates of *perception*, and investigate how far it could be suggested that a disembodied person might perceive. Then I shall try to evaluate the suggestion that a disembodied person might continue to exercise *agency*. The choice is dictated by two considerations. The content which can be given to the notion of disembodied personality will derive mainly from the alleged capacity of the disembodied to continue to have experiences. And the recourse to disembodied personality as an explanation of alleged paranormal phenomena is bound to involve the claim that disembodied persons are performing actions in our world. In other respects, these notions will raise questions that are typical of those that would arise if other predicates were considered.

Let us begin our consideration of the vocabulary of perception by taking the language of *vision*. Could a disembodied person be said without absurdity to *see*? If one is inclined to say 'Yes' to this question, one incurs the obligation to give some account of what it is to see when one cannot look at what one sees, walk up to what one sees, or avoid colliding with it. Clearly the only hope for such an account is to begin immediately to do what many post-Cartesian epistemologists tried to do, and attempt to define what it is for this sort of being to see in terms of his having certain *visual experiences*. There need be nothing viciously circular in this, however; for we are in a position to assume what the classical epistemologist could not assume but was often trying subsequently to demonstrate—that there is a physical world to be seen, that there are many observers with eyes in that world to see it, and that they do see parts of it frequently. We can then proceed as follows. A disembodied person might have a visual field in which the objects set before him were arranged in the pattern in which they would be arranged for a normal observer in optimum circumstances viewing those objects from a particular position in space. This could perhaps be put less questionbeggingly as follows: there seems no difficulty in saying of a disembodied person that it might look to him as though there were objects before him which looked to him as they would look to a normal observer under optimum circumstances from a certain position in space. I feel obliged to start from some such account as this because I can attach no sense to the notion of seeing from no point of view, or seeing non-perspectivally. Given the intelligibility of this story, and given that there *are* objects in space arranged as stated, it seems quite pedantic to deny, does it not, that our disembodied person *sees* them? So let us say he does.

We must now face the question of whether or not to say that our disembodied person, having this visual experience, is himself in space. He does not fill any part of it—or at least not in the normal way that precludes anything else from filling it at the same time. But there is some temptation to say nevertheless that he is in it, just because he sees things that are in it. I shall proceed for the moment on the assumption that we decide to say he *is* in space, and will return later to the consequences of saying he is not. If he is in space, he must be *somewhere* in it. Where? We may not *know* where, of course, but still if he is in it he must be somewhere in it. The only non-arbitrary way of answering the question is this: we have to say that the disembodied person is at the place from which, when a normal observer sees the objects which our survivor now sees, they look to that observer the way they look to our survivor. Roughly, he has to be at the centre of his visual field.

The first thing that seems to follow is that his seeing things the way he does cannot be construed as a *consequence* of his being where he is, for his being where he is *consists in* his seeing things the way he does. Even if it is not a necessary condition of A's being said to cause B that A and B should be identifiable independently, it is surely a necessary condition of our saying that A causes B that we are able to say without contradiction that one might occur without the other even if in fact it does not; and this condition is not satisfied here.

The second thing that seems to follow is that it is logically impossible to say of him that things look, at least in their grosser features, different to him from the way they look to most people. Nothing that he sees can look to him different from the way it *really looks*. For we have said that he is at a certain position; and this position is the position where they really look the way they look to him. If they do not look to him the way they really look, then there is nowhere that we can say that he is.

These points may seem minor. Perhaps we do not care whether we can apply to a disembodied being the distinction between how things look to him and how they really look, or look to most people. What about the much more important distinction between the way things look and the way they really are? Can he use it, and can it be used of him? As a survivor, he has presumably inherited the distinction, in the form of certain beliefs about how things are. Such beliefs would enable him at times to discount the way things looked to him. If he did sometimes discount how they looked, and fell back on these inherited beliefs about how they were, and they really were the way he decided they were, then he would presumably both have and use the distinction between how things look and how they are. It seems pedantic to deny it.

But as we have described his situation so far, he has to depend on applying an inherited notion and falling back on inherited beliefs and happening, fortuitously, to be right. Now this can perhaps be described as correcting misleading perceptions. But any being restricted to this would be in the very weakest epistemological position. For we have not supplied in our account an element which is commonly available when people are said to be able to correct misleading perceptions, viz. the capacity to do this because one gets less misleading ones. And this ability to get less misleading ones seems in turn connected with the capacity to *set out to get* the less misleading ones. Can the disembodied being have these abilities and so have something rather closer than we have so far supplied to the embodied person's ability to correct his perceptions?

To start with, it does seem possible to imagine a being who can correct misleading perceptions by making the proper use of non-misleading ones which he gets, without being able to set out to get non-misleading ones. We can imagine a man strapped down to a hospital bed, with neck and eye muscles paralysed, so that he can do nothing more than stare fixedly in one direction. Let us add to this that he retains his commonsense knowledge of the world from his more fortunate earlier years. Such a person could sometimes get percept p-1, be unsure whether what he saw really was the way that p-1 made it look, and then be fortunate enough to get percept p-2 which he took to be more reliable than p-1; and he could happen to be right about this judgment. He might see the nurse pass by twice nearer the second time than the first, and thereby be able to correct his earlier impression that her hair is red and decide, correctly, that it is blonde. So as long as someone is able to make the correct epistemic use of his perceptions, it is possible logically for him to be able to apply the distinction between how things look and how they are without being able to seek out, or set out to get, improved perceptions: he might manage by being very clever about the ones he happens to get. Obviously, of course, such a person would be very handicapped indeed in the knowledge he could acquire, and his perceptual judgments would be very hazardous. (One of the things that would reduce the hazard of them would be his own knowledge of his physical situation.) In the case of a disembodied person, it might indeed be that he could correctly use the distinction between how things looked and how they were in an analogous way, and might be said to correct misleading perceptions on the basis of better ones he happened to get. Let us now ask whether the epistemological hazardousness of this situation could be relieved by our ascribing to him the capacity to seek out better visual perceptions.

In our own case, of course, we usually do this by moving about until we can see better, look carefully, or peer. For a disembodied person looking and peering are rather obviously out of the question. Can he move? We can say that he can move if we define this carefully: if we understand the word 'move' merely to mean first being in one position (defined as previously) and then being in another position. This, of course, is only movement in the sense of passage from one position in space to another. It is not, thus far at least, deliberate movement; it is not *moving oneself*. It is this latter that we need, to reach any legitimate talk about setting out to get a better view of something, rather than just receiving it. How are we to give sense to the notion of the disembodied person deliberately moving from one place to another? We cannot give sense to this by reference to the movement of his limbs, for he has none; nor to sensations of muscular strain, for even if he has these they will be illusory. We have to try to give a purely introspective, mental sense to it, which is on the face of it obscure. We are now confronted with a problem which I will consider in more detail shortly in discussing agency; I will be rather brief with it at our present stage. How, then, can we give a purely mental sense to the notion of deliberately moving to see better?

The only possible way seems to be to try to define this in terms of deciding or trying or willing, followed by: the better percept. The trouble with this is that 'deciding' or 'trying' or 'willing' (which I take here to be a philosophical technicality roughly equivalent to 'deciding' or 'trying') are incomplete expressions. To understand the claim that someone is deciding or trying I have to have some notion of what it is that he is deciding or trying to do; better, for it to be true that someone is trying or deciding it has also to be the case that there is something that he is deciding or trying to do, even if I can at times tell from the sweat on his brow that he is trying to do something without being able to say exactly what it is. But what is it that our disembodied person in our story is trying or deciding to do? Answer: to *get* a better view. Not, notice, to *have* a better view, for this last is not something that one does, but something that happens to one, and therefore is not something that one can in logic precede by trying or deciding, because it is not an action. But the trouble with saying that what one is trying or deciding to do is to get a better view is that this is the very notion that we were trying to define. It turns out that the notions we are tempted to use for the purpose are not simple introspective notions, and cannot supply what we need. But let us put this problem, temporarily, on one side. Let us suppose we can give simple introspective sense to the idea of a disembodied person's trying to move, or trying to be somewhere other than he is. We then face another difficulty. If it makes sense to say that a disembodied being might be somewhere else than the place he is in, merely by trying to be, then there seems no reason to deny that the notion makes sense as applied to an embodied person. But in fact no embodied person is able to do this. If we came across someone who was able to do this, we would say that he had special, probably miraculous powers. So it seems that in order to give sense to the notion of a disembodied person's being able to get a better view of something we have to ascribe to him special powers that you and I do not have, viz. powers of changing his position in space merely by trying to do so.

An objection is natural here. It might be said that it is much less tempting to call movement by mere trying miraculous in the disembodied person's case than in ours, because we have bodies and he does not. He therefore, to put the matter crudely, has so much less to move than we do. To deal with this objection I will try to describe the situation of the disembodied person with more care. We have defined his occupying a position in terms of his having a certain visual field, viz. the one that a normal observer in that position would have. So all that changing his position in space would come to would be his changing the visual field for another, better one. What we have to try to supply for him in our story is the ability to bring *this* about deliberately, when he cannot do it by peering or squinting or putting on bifocals, or walking. He has to be able to change his visual field *just by trying to*. But *this* is something that embodied persons cannot do. So to give the disembodied person the power to change his visual field deliberately, which we need to do to give him the power to correct his perceptions by getting better ones, we have to give him a special power that you or I do not have.

Someone may now say that we do have this power. We can, sometimes, change our visual field merely by concentrating on it in a particular way. We do this in the case of ambiguous pictures, at least when we are told what can be seen in them if we try; we also can do it by staring over and over at a picture and suddenly becoming aware of some element that we missed before. These cases give some content to the notion of perceptual change being consequent solely upon mental effort. My point must then be reworded: a disembodied person who could by this means get a better view would have this familiar power *enormously extended*, extended to produce changes in the grossest features of his visual field. Perhaps, of course, death may release this power in the way Plato suggested it released our intellectual powers. Whether or not this idea seems attractive to anyone, the fact remains that something like this would have to be ascribed to a disembodied person if that person were to be said to be able to correct his visual perceptions by more than the use of better percepts he receives fortuitously.

Thus far we have been proceeding on the assumption that our disembodied person is to be said to have spatial position. Suppose we abandon this. Let us say, then, that he sees (in the manner we have defined) without saying that he is therefore at the place from which an ordinary observer would be seeing if he saw the way our disembodied observer sees. More briefly, we can say that our disembodied observer sees *clairvoyantly*, since clairvoyant seeing, I believe, is seeing without being in a position to see, or something like this. Suppose, now, our disembodied clairvoyant observer wonders whether some object really is as it now looks to him to be, and wants a better view of it. Can he deliberately get one? The answer seems to be as before, without the irrelevant preliminaries about movement: yes, he can get a better view, if we give him the power to have a better percept by trying to have one. This is, surely, super-clairvoyance, and even if non-super clairvoyance is not a special power, this surely is. Failing the possession of this special power, our disembodied person would be restricted, for the purpose of correcting his perceptions, to the recognition of those better clairvoyant percepts that he was lucky enough to receive fortuitously.

So much for vision. Let us consider *hearing*. I incline to think the position is roughly analogous. There seems no good reason, if we ascribe to a disembodied person the experience of the sounds that a normal listener would hear at a given spot, to refuse to say that he hears what such a normal listener would hear, and is at the spot where that ordinary listener would hear it. If we locate him in space in this way, we cannot say that what he hears sounds different to him from the way it sounds to others. He can, through the use of his inherited pre-mortem beliefs, use the distinction between how things sound to be and how they are. He can be said to correct his auditory perception by making judgments about the sounds he hears and other less misleading sounds he happens to hear. But he can only be said to follow a corrective auditory procedure if he has the ability to hear better by the mere exercise of auditory concentration. This ability would either have to be a special power, or a special extension of an existing power. Failing one or other of these, he would not be in a position to correct his hearing other than through the correct interpretations of sounds he happened to hear fortuitously.

A few comments now about *other senses*. A disembodied person could not have perceptions of his own bodily states, for obvious reasons. So any sense given to the claim that he can have any particular form of sense-perception must exclude this. This does not exclude *any sensations*, of course, as long as these are not said to be perceptions of bodily states. Sensations like tickles or glows, for example, might occur, and even be informative; just not informative about the state of the percipient's body, since he does not have one. They could be informative about other things; or we might reasonably be tempted to say so. For example, if a disembodied person felt the sensation that we have when a feather touches our skin, we might say of him that it feels to him as though there is a feather touching him, although we (and one hopes he) know that he cannot be touched; and that since there is a feather at about the right distance from where he is (this being defined as we defined it before) this sensation is veridical as far as the contour of the edge of the feather is concerned. A glow might well be illusory in that it felt as though the temperature of the body which he does not have was rising, but might be veridical in that it also suggested to him, correctly, that the temperature of the room had risen. So we could give a suitably antiseptic sense, perhaps, to the idea of a *sense of touch* for a disembodied person. He could not *touch* anything, but he might be said to learn about it *by touch*, or tactually, in that it might feel rough or warm to him, when it *was* rough or warm. I forbear to enter once again into the special powers that would be involved in his correcting his tactile sensations. I have no doubt that the hypothesis of disembodied touch is much more uninviting than that of disembodied hearing or vision. The reason for this is that touch is one of the senses that normally affects not only the percipient but also what he perceives. So if the disembodied person learns about the contour of the feather in the way described it has to be added that the edge of the feather is in no way and to no degree indented when he does. Similar considerations seem to fit smell and taste. Though he could not sniff, or roll his tongue, or smack his lips, a disembodied person just might be said to smell or taste by having olfactory or gustatory sensations, which, though illusorily suggesting bodily contact with the objects of these senses, did yield correct judgments about their being sour or rotten or stale. Again, being able to improve on this would entail having special powers. And the relevant experiences would have to occur without there being any ingestion of particles from the surfaces of the objects smelled or tasted. Someone might say: to give a disembodied person these capacities you are giving him a body back surreptitiously. This is not so. If he had his body back he would see it again; and he does not. If he had his body back the tickles and glows would be indications of bodily disturbances near the skin; and they are not. And if he had his body back, it would fill the space that other objects occupy; and it does not.

To sum up: there seems no decisive reason to insist that a disembodied person could not perceive our world, or, with the aid of inherited true beliefs about its nature, make some correct judgments about it, and be able to understand and sometimes correctly use, the fundamental distinction between how it seems and how it is. Failing the addition of special powers of control over his perceptions, however, he would not be able to attain to adequate assurance on how things actually were to anything like the extent to which an embodied person can. This would not prevent his having beliefs about what was taking place in the world, or feeling emotions or attitudes to it. Emotions and attitudes usually have objects, of course; but this requirement can be supplied in this case through the disembodied person's awareness of the things and persons of which he is still conscious.

His emotions and attitudes would run the risk of being ill-founded to the extent to which his information about the world is inadequate. Furthermore, their *expression* would be circumscribed. Although the disembodied person could imagine the object of his fear to be absent, as we all do in wishful moments, he could not run from it; though perhaps the above discussion might permit us to give some intelligible account of his *moving away* from it. (But then, what would he have to fear from it?) Although he could easily enough imagine with glee that some calamity was overtaking the object of his anger, he would not be able to strike the blow himself as you or I could. This kind of possibility, however, depends on the possibility of disembodied agency.

CHAPTER 3

DISEMBODIED AGENCY

WHAT would be involved in saying of some strange happening that it was in fact something which a disembodied person had *done*? Suppose, for example, that we are at a seance and a table rises; and it is suggested that this is because a spirit raised it; and a spirit is supposed to be a disembodied person. To parody a famous question from Wittgenstein, 'What is left over when we subtract the fact that the table rose from the fact that the spirit raised the table?'

There must *be* more to the spirit's raising the table than the table's rising, self-evidently; but the more that there is cannot be identical with the more that there is when an embodied person raises the table—this includes such things as his putting his hands under the table and exerting upward pressure. Now whatever strength the temptation to say that the difference between its rising and its being raised lies in some mental act has in the case of ordinary, embodied agents the strength of the temptation is obviously increased in the case of disembodied agents. What else, after all, could be difference consist in? We seem forced to say that the difference between 'The spirit raised the table' and 'The table rose' must lie in some mental act that precedes the rising of the table. This mental act will provide a partial analogue to the physical performances that embodied agents have to go through when they set out to raise things.

Notice first one or two consequences of the fact that when embodied agents raise tables they have to go through certain physical performances to do it. Firstly, it is by reference to these that we understand a notion like 'trying to lift the table': this I would do if I placed my hands underneath it and heaved; if nothing happened I would have tried and failed; if it rose I would have tried and succeeded. It is also by reference to these that we understand the notion of deciding to lift the table: of course, I can decide to lift it without deciding to do it *this way*, but to decide to do it is to decide to do it *somehow*, to go through whatever procedures seem necessary: if I do not go through any of them I have changed my mind. 'Willing' in the technical sense seems to be in the same position as deciding is. All of them are incomplete, also: to try, decide, or will, one has to try, decide, or will *to do so-and-so*, so to say that someone is trying or deciding or willing is to make use of the notion of action already. (One can, actually, decide that a table should rise: but this merely means that one can decide to do whatever will make it rise, and we still use the notion of action here. And one cannot even make sense of the phrase 'trying that the table rise' as opposed to 'trying to raise the table.') All of this suggests that we are not in a position to say that the analogue for the embodied person's physical performances that precede the rising of the table when a disembodied person raises a table will consist in his trying or deciding or willing, in the technical sense; for these notions lean on, and do not serve to explain, the notion of doing.

There is a chance, though: for there is another rather obscure but familiar enough sense of 'willing'. It is roughly equivalent to privately urging something to happen that I want to happen, even though it cannot pay heed to me. A handy example is given using psychokinetic experiments. Here dice are shaken and thrown by machines, and subjects are told to will a certain score, say double-six. It is alleged that the results are statistically significant. If they are, this suggests a mysterious power that some people have to affect the course of nature by willing: the task is then to investigate whatever laws govern this mysterious power. I think this sort of willing is familiar. But unlike the technical sort of willing, which is supposed to precede some or all free actions according to some philosophers, the psychokinetic sort of willing is itself in action. To discover that dice will fall double-six because we will for double-six is to discover that when I do this action, certain natural results will follow. It is like finding out that when the magician says 'Abracadabra, let X happen', X *does* happen. Now willing in this sense might perhaps be the required analogue of the placing of hands and heaving that embodied agents have to go through. It might be that this sort of willing was the sort of procedure that a disembodied person had to go through to raise tables, and the like. I need hardly say that this would be a special power, or, if the psychokinetic experiments prosper, it might be the extension of an ordinary power. Can we use the notion of such a power, and can we use this notion of spirit agency, to explain things like tables rising? Perhaps, though only, I suspect, if we can give sense to correlating degrees of this power with magnitude of elevation, weight of objects lifted, and like things. And one could always wonder why the power had to be assigned to a spirit rather than to some embodied person in the room.

I think it is worth while here to come at this question another way, through the terminology of *basic actions*, which Arthur Danto has introduced.[1] In using it I shall have to change it slightly, because I think his introduction of it is not the most convenient possible way. Danto distinguishes between two kinds of action, basic and non-basic. Basic actions are actions not caused by some other action of the agent who does them; non-basic actions are actions that are the effects of causal chains originating with basic actions. He argues that if there are any actions, there must be basic actions; if there were not, no one could ever begin to act. As an example of a non-basic action he gives the moving of a stone. I can only produce the motion of the stone by doing something (e.g. kicking it) which causes the stone to move. He says further that every normal person has the same repertoire of basic actions. Some, however, can do as basic actions things that the rest of us can only do as non-basic actions, e.g. (my example) wiggling one's ears: he calls them positively abnormal people. Others are unable to do, except perhaps as non-basic actions, things that are basic actions to the rest of us, e.g. the paralytic who cannot raise his arm except perhaps by lifting it with the other arm: he calls them negatively abnormal people. All agents, he says, have *some* repertoire of basic actions. If an action is basic we cannot give any-

[1] Arthur Danto, 'Basic Actions', and elsewhere.

one a description of how to do it, because there is nothing to do *first*. Finally, it is only possible to do something *just by trying* if it is a basic action.

I would suggest the following amendment to this very useful account. Critics have noticed that the causal model seems confusing as the basis for the distinction between basic and non-basic actions. If I move the stone by kicking it there is something I have to do (the kicking) to move the stone; but the relationship is not causal. What is caused by my kicking the stone is the stone's moving, not my moving it. Further, there seem to be cases we would intuitively class as non-basic, such as the knotting of a tie.[1] Here the whole action seems to be the sum-total of a series of basic actions, not to be something distinct from them which they cause. Because of these difficulties in Danto's way of formulating the distinction, I would suggest instead that we define a basic action as follows. An action is a basic action for someone if there is no other action which he has to do in order to do that action. Although I do not know how to demonstrate it, it seems to follow from this definition that there are only two major sorts of basic actions for people on this definition: mental actions, like imagining or saying to oneself, and movements of one's own limbs or members. For any action like raising a table, that involves action *upon* physical things, is something that one has to move one's limbs or members to do.

To return now to our disembodied agent. I have argued, in effect, and can now do so explicitly, that moving a table is not a basic action for us, and that there is necessarily something, or some things, that we

[1] Myles Brand, 'Danto on Basic Actions'.

have to do first in order to do it. In our case it is the movement of the hands and arms. In the case of the disembodied agent there must be some analogue of this, and this will be the mental act of willing, or the recitation of some formula. To give him the capacity to exercise agency in the world, we have to give him this special power to bring things about in this manner.

But, it might be said, why does there have to be an analogue to the physical movements that embodied agents have to go through? Why not just say that moving things is a basic action for a disembodied person? Would he not have a different repertoire of basic actions from the rest of us? Yes, this could be said. But notice two things. First, this, too, would be a special power—disembodied persons that can move tables are 'positively abnormal'. Second, if I agree to say that raising a table could be a basic action for a spirit, then I shall feel strongly tempted to say that the table, at least at the time when it is raised, becomes temporarily the body of the spirit. For in order to say the raising of the table is a basic action one has to say that there is no need for willing or formula-reciting, because there is nothing the spirit has to do in order to raise the table. But then the analogy with the physical movements of the embodied person's body is as close as it can be, and why not draw the conclusion?

If one were willing to draw it, it would have another interesting result. The cases which tend to arouse the most interest among psychical researchers are not the cases where spirits are alleged to move physical objects, but cases where they are alleged to communicate by speaking through the mouths of mediums. If one can contemplate with calm the possibility of spirits occu-

pying physical objects, there seems no great obstacle
to contemplating with equal calm the possibility of
their occupying the bodies of embodied persons for
short periods: periods during which the person whose
body it is appears not to be in possession of her facul-
ties but to be, as we might say, absent; in a trance. If
this were so, then the medium would indeed merely be
what she says she is, a temporary mouthpiece for the
spirit. Whether the fact that our argument ends up
where the spiritualist would like to start is a good thing,
I shall not try to say. Instead I shall sum up with a
few more general reflections.

Just as, with many provisos, it does not seem impossible to suggest that a disembodied person could
perceive the world, I have not uncovered any reasons
for saying that such a person could not act in it. Our
reluctance to say that it could is probably due to the
fact, which I would claim to have shown, that there is
something necessarily occult or magical about the idea
of such disembodied agency. This conclusion is hardly
surprising, but it might serve at least to give our com-
mon-sense suspicions some logical, rather than aesthetic, grounds. We can comfort ourselves with the fact
that one would never *have* to say that an object
moved because a spirit moved it; we could always rest
on saying, if ordinary explanations failed us, that some
embodied person present had psychokinetic powers—
perhaps unconscious ones. This person might, of
course, be the medium. But the most this shows is that
we can comfortingly relegate the spirit-stories once
again to the realm of fantasy. It does not show that
they are unintelligible. To show this much more is
needed. One possible way of doing it is to resort once

again to arguments deriving from considerations about self-identity. For to talk about spirits having temporary embodiments or exercising causal powers assumes that we can think of them as persisting as single non-physical entities through time, entities that can perhaps pass out of one body into another. But on this, for the present, I have elected a self-denying ordinance. It is enough to show that any demonstration of the absurdity of the notion of disembodied agency must come, indeed, from that more general source.

CHAPTER 4

THE NEXT WORLD

IN order to investigate the extent to which we can give content to the notion of disembodied personality we have examined the possible use of concepts of perception and agency. It was taken for granted that if a disembodied person sees or hears, what he sees or hears will be objects (things, persons) that an embodied person would see or hear; and that if a disembodied person can perform actions, these would include, in addition to mental actions, actions that bring about changes in our physical world. It seemed a matter of choice whether or not to say that his seeing things in space, or acting on them, implied his having a spatial position; but it seems natural, even so, to say that we have proceeded so far as though the disembodied survivor would inhabit the world that we inhabit. The assumption is natural enough: for how else could he have anything to perceive, or anything to do? But this assumption has only to be made explicit to be shown to be questionable. It would be a strange discussion of survival indeed that did not include some consideration of the possibility that those who survive death survive in *another* world, not in this one.

This possibility, on the other hand, runs the risk of

being, for us, an empty one. For references to the
Next World cannot be intelligible for us unless it is
possible to use the language of our world of things and
persons to 'describe it. And only if references to it
are intelligible can we understand the claim that a
survivor might perceive or act in it. So the chance of
giving content to the belief that after death one survives, disembodied, in another world, depends on our
being able to articulate the concept of the Next World
in the language of this one.

One obvious way of doing this is to say that the
Next World, though numerically distinct from this
world, is nevertheless a spatial world with physical
objects in it. The theory of another world that is
spatial and contains physical objects, but is not in
Space is dauntingly counter-intuitive, but I cannot explore its difficulties here. If we were able to overcome
them, then the difficulty of articulating the notions of
disembodied perception and agency and the like for
that world would be much the same as that of articulating the same notions for *this* one. And we have already dealt with this. On the other hand, any difficulty
there may be associated with the belief that one enters
the Next World from this one *in* the body must be
postponed until we consider the doctrine of resurrection; and it is clearly likely to be a difficulty about the
identifying of the person so entering with one of us.
But there is another possibility, more in accord perhaps
with the general tenor of belief in disembodied survival.
It is the possibility that the Next World, and the disembodied persons 'in' it, are not in space at all, either
this or another.

But if the Next World is not in space, how can there

be anything in the Next World to perceive or to do?
How can one say at all what the Next World, so conceived, would be like? However unpromising an enterprise it might seem to be to answer this question, an
answer of great ingenuity and persuasiveness has been
offered by Professor H. H. Price.[1]

Failing the existence of perceptible physical objects
in an environment that the disembodied survivor would
occupy, the content of such a survivor's experience has
to be spun from within. Whatever we say of disembodied existence, the inner activity of imagination,
which has no organ, is something a survivor might very
well be expected to continue. Price suggests, therefore,
that our survivor who is out of space could have a life
which consists in sequences of *images*. He claims that
the experience of a disembodied survivor, not in our
space, can contain many analogies of our ordinary
perceptual experience, because of the significance that
would come to be attached to certain kinds of image
sequences. In his very suggestive development of this
hypothesis, Price makes use of the generic notion of
having images, introducing for it the term 'imaging'.
Certain key elements in his account depend on the
legitimacy of his doing this. He says there might be
analogues of the perception of one's own body for the
disembodied person: there might 'be' a cluster of
appropriate 'body'-images—presumably present in-
voluntarily. There might also be an apparent environment which might be changed voluntarily, as one
changes one's imagined surroundings in daydreams.
These voluntary and involuntary experiences together

[1] H. H. Price, 'Survival and the Idea of "Another World" ', and
'What kind of Next World?'

form the 'world' of the survivor. He argues it would be wrong to say that the Next World, if it consisted of experiences of this kind, would be illusory; for the images would, for the survivor, *be there*, and would therefore constitute the only reality which his world could have.

Now there are at least some philosophical objections to speaking of images collectively in this way. Malcolm, for example, has argued against the very natural philosophical inference that because we dream that some events occur, there must therefore be an actual sequence of image-events that really does occur in our experience.[1] Ryle has argued against a similar inference in the case of imagining.[2] Munsat has pointed out some of the dangers that lie in wait for us if we do not distinguish one kind of imagining from another with enough care.[3] If their arguments have force (and I shall not explore them here) they would tend to make us wary of Price's last suggestion about the reality of the Next World, for this depends upon severing the talk of images from its normal connections with the language of dreaming, imagining, or hallucinating. But it is not at all clear that in speaking of having images we are saying anything more or less than that we are dreaming or imagining or hallucinating. Except, of course, that in staying with the generic expression we refrain from saying *which* of these things we are doing. This very imprecision makes it easy to be lulled into accepting the suggestion that one is doing *none* of them. Yet if one is having involuntary images and is

[1] Norman Malcolm, *Dreaming*.
[2] Gilbert Ryle, *The Concept of Mind*, Chapter VIII.
[3] Stanley Munsat, *The Concept of Memory*, Chapter VI.

not (*ex hypothesi*) perceiving, then one is presumably dreaming or hallucinating, whereas if one is having voluntary images, or controlling one's images at will, yet not perceiving, one is presumably imagining or daydreaming. So there can be nothing more to the suggestion that the world of images is for our survivors the *real* world than the claim that imagining or dreaming or hallucinating is, in default of there being objects in an environment to perceive, all that these survivors can do. This suggestion, though, is right enough.

It is not certain that all of these possibilities are open. In particular, the language of dreaming seems odd for a being that cannot sleep. And certain customary associations of the notions that remain would have to be abandoned—such as the suggestion that a hallucination can be combined with a genuine perception (that I have a hallucination of a pink rat on the mantelpiece which I see). But in view of the fact that such activities as imagining and hallucinating do not have organs that we do them with, as sight and hearing do, it seems pedantic to suggest that we could not intelligibly ascribe at least a reduced number of such mental performances to the survivor. If these were, for example, hallucinating (for the involuntary cases) and imagining (for the voluntary cases) we would probably have an adequate vocabulary in terms of which the language of imaging could be understood. The fact, however, that it had to be understood in these terms would serve to remind us that the survivor does not perceive, but that his world is private. We are speaking here, of course, of what *we* can properly say *about* such a survivor. It is quite in order to suggest, as Price does, that he might come to give his inherited language of perception a *new use*, to describe to himself the imaginary and hallucinatory experiences he has.

As Price explains, this could come about in the following way. There might be a cluster of persistent visual images, presumably involuntary, that came to constitute an image-body. There would be no body, indeed no environment, but the survivor might have involuntary images *of* such a body. These need not all be visual: if we allow tactile and kinaesthetic hallucinations, disembodiment might seem very like embodiment is. Furthermore, there might be involuntary images of a non-existent environment, so that although the survivor would not be in space, he might have the imaginative illusion that he was. We then have the materials necessary for the private use in this image-world of all the concepts of perception that we use now.

Price adds a further suggestion of great interest: that the Next World might be a wish-fulfilment world. Wishes for certain events might be followed, as in daydreams, by the images of those events. The wish to be at a certain place might be followed by the images of that place. In other words, in the absence of a real environment, the survivor's imagination might create its own private one. On the surface this would seem to be the place where we would make use of the concept of voluntary imaging. But in the case of deeper wish-fulfilments, where the wishes are unconscious or unacknowledged, the images would not be under *conscious* control. It might rather be that in some cases there were hallucinatory experiences generated by unconscious or unacknowledged wishes. It might be here that a survivor reaped the benefits or suffered the penalties of the character he had built up during life.

The involuntary images, whether due to unconscious wishes or not, might *to him* come to be events that happened to him in his (hallucinatory) environment, whereas the sequences of images under voluntary control might *to him* come to be his actions in and upon that environment. We need not explore whether if they come to be these things to him he could still retain his normal concept of imagining. But we now, constructing this fantasy about him, can say of him only that he would be living an existence of imaginings and hallucinations.

With these provisos, there seems (again, if we put aside questions of knowledge and identity) no insuperable obstacle to the construction of a logically viable notion of disembodied survival out of space. The account we have constructed, following Price, has two difficulties.

First and far more serious, is the Next World not a solipsistic world? Although no disembodied person could perceive another, in a world in which survivors could perceive embodied persons, they would have the same reason to believe in the existence of other disembodied persons as those embodied persons had. Scanty though this seems to be, it might include allegedly paranormal manifestations of disembodied agency. But in the Next World as we have now described it the survivor could perceive no thing or person whatever. This does not mean that he could not have, among the images in his experience, images 'of' other persons, but whatever they would come to mean to him they could not be perceptions of other disembodied survivors, since those survivors could have no perceptible characteristics. It is conceivable, of course, that the images that one survivor had of other persons were closely similar to the images that certain other survivors in fact had for their image-bodies. It might not be wholly outrageous to construe this as perception; but nothing short of pre-established harmony could account for its occurrence, as Leibniz and perhaps Berkeley understood. For Smith's mind may contain images of Jones, but it cannot contain Jones himself.

It is tempting to say the same thing about the logical possibility of our disembodied survivor's perceiving embodied persons or physical things. Suppose it were the case, as we have so far assumed it is not, that some reasonably lengthy sequence of physical-object-images is interpreted by its owner as a perception of some part of our world, and that there is, by coincidence, just such a part of our world that is arranged the way the contents of his image-world look to him to be arranged? Might not this fortuitously veridical hallucination be called *seeing*? And would not some doctrine of pre-established harmony be the only way of explaining it? One must certainly answer 'Yes' to the first question, and probably to the second. But the situation envisaged in the first is the one with which we began the investigation of disembodied perception, since this is the only definition of seeing for disembodied persons open to us. At this point our former and our present accounts of the survivor's world are not clearly distinguishable. And it is important to remember that even in our account of disembodied perception where we assumed that the survivor perceived things and persons in this world, no suggestion was offered of how he could come to do so. To maintain the purity of the second hypothesis,

then, the survivor must not be allowed to perceive
this world from the Next one. His images, that is,
must either not correspond to any vistas in this world,
or not be thought by their owner to be perceptions
of it.

This brings us to our second, and less serious,
difficulty. In our earlier account of disembodied agency
it was tacitly assumed that any interference by disembodied agents in our world would be the consequence of their perception of it. If this is not
admitted into the hypothesis, then it is hard to see
how any event in this world can be ascribed to someone in the Next except as an utterly mysterious cosmic
accident, unknown even to its perpetrator. The inutility for psychical researchers of this sort of possibility, in contrast to that which we explored before,
is clear.

CHAPTER 5

MEMORY AND PERSONAL IDENTITY

WE have spoken of the disembodied person performing actions and having experiences. Most
of these last through short or long stretches of time.
To be entitled to speak in this way we have to be able
to make intelligible to ourselves the continued existence of such a disembodied being through time. We
have also spoken of this disembodied being inheriting
certain abilities from his pre-mortem state. To be
entitled to speak of this we have to be able to make
intelligible to ourselves the identity of this person with
some previous embodied person. So we need some way
of understanding the identity of the disembodied being
through various post-mortem stages, and some way of
understanding the statement that some such being is
identical with one particular pre-mortem being rather
than with another. We shall not be able to understand
either unless we can also understand the notion of the
numerical difference between one such disembodied
being and another one.

A natural and tempting line of argument is the
following. We obviously cannot say that Smith (disembodied) at time T_1 and Smith (disembodied) at
time T_2 are identical because of their possession of the

same body, or of any physical characteristics. But it is easy to say what would make them one and the same disembodied person. It would be the fact that Smith at T_2 has memories that reach back to, and encompass, the experiences of Smith at T_1. And what makes Smith at T_2 identical with Smith at T_1 rather than with Jones at T_1 is that Smith at T_2 has memories that encompass the experiences of Smith at T_1 but not those of Jones at T_1. Further, what makes Smith at T_1 and Smith at T_2 identical with pre-mortem Smith, is the same: the memories the post-mortem Smith has encompass the doings and experiences of the pre-mortem Smith and not those of the pre-mortem Jones.

This line of argument itself invites an equally natural and tempting counter-argument. Memories are, notoriously, fallible. It is clearly not plausible to say that Smith's memories of some past event show that event to have been part of his life-history. On the contrary, we can only plausibly allege that his memory beliefs show this if we know that he has a *good* memory, not a bad one. We have to know that his memories are *real*, not merely apparent. The word 'remember' is ambiguous, and has a strong and a weak sense. In the strong sense to say that someone remembers p is to commit oneself to the truth of p, and to say that he remembers doing a or experiencing e is to say that he indeed did do a or experience e. In the weak sense, to say that someone remembers is to say merely that he claims, or believes himself, to remember in the strong sense. Someone can, then, in the weak sense, remember without its being true that p exists or that he did a, or that he experienced e. In the weak sense one can *mis*-remember, in the strong sense only *fail to* remember, which one can do in one way by thinking that one remembers when one does not. The talk of 'memories' in the previous account of disembodied identity is ambiguous between these two senses. For the thesis to succeed the memories referred to have to be real memories, i.e. memories in the strong sense. This requires that we should be able to distinguish between those occasions when what someone thinks he remembers actually happened to him, and those occasions when they did not. This we cannot do in terms of his recollections themselves. There has to be some independent way of determining that the person who did or experienced what Smith believes he remembers doing or experiencing was, or was not, Smith himself. And this, it seems, has to be his physical presence at the occasion in question. So memory is not an independent standard of identity. Without the possibility of recourse to the bodily presence of the person at some past time we are unable to understand what it would be like to determine that some event or action is, or is not, part of this person's past life. So we would have no standard of identity to use of a disembodied person at all.

I think this refutation is in essence correct, and does contain within it enough to put out of the question an intelligible concept of disembodied survival. But in order to show this it is necessary to deal with certain difficulties that derive from the literature on personal identity, and to refine the argument both to take account of these, and to deal with the special problems that face us when we are discussing the identity of disembodied persons, not the identity of persons in general. It is sometimes said that to put the problems of personal identity in terms of the relation between *two* standards of identity, since there are a number, is misleading. It has been said that an argument like the one outlined suggests that our reliance on people's memories in disputes about their identity is merely inductively based, when it is not. It has been said that one can construct imaginary examples (or even find real ones) which strongly tempt us to concede that someone's memory-beliefs might have priority over the continuity of his body, so that we might feel forced to admit the possibility, in logic, of bodily transfer or reincarnation. I have already listed some of these examples. If they show what they are alleged to show, it might seem that there is no absurdity in the claim that a person's identity could depend entirely on his memories. Finally, our argument is couched in terms that suggest it is at bottom an epistemological one. It seems to amount merely to the claim that we could not *know* whether a disembodied being was or was not identical with some past disembodied or embodied being. But we have put aside parallel epistemological considerations in dealing with problems about pre-dication, in order to avoid making conceptual decisions hinge upon issues of very high philosophical generality. Might they not be put aside here? Surely the question is whether we can *understand* the belief that dis-embodied persons last through time, not one about how we would *know* that one had done so? In order to deal with these difficulties I must turn first to a more general discussion of self-identity, and apply the results later to our special case.

In a general discussion of self-identity it is not possible to avoid epistemological considerations, since in outlining the rules of application for an expression like 'the same person' one is bound to ask in what circumstances users (and learners) of our language are able to tell whether to apply it or withhold it, and this is, in the broadest sense, an epistemological question. (This does not prevent our going on to ask how far a doctrine like that of disembodied survival, which postulates conditions in which our language could not be learned, and in which no one would know whether or not the conditions that justified the use of the expression actually obtained, could be intelligibly expressed in our language, if its possession is taken as given.)

Confining ourselves to the conventions we now follow in our talk of flesh-and-blood persons (rather than the conventions we might come to follow if certain philosophical fantasies like those of Locke came true), I would suggest that both bodily identity and memory are criteria of personal identity. By saying they are criteria of personal identity I mean the following. (i) It follows from the fact that a person, Y, now before us, has the body that a person, X, previously known, had, that Y is X. (ii) It follows from the fact that a person, Y, now before us, remembers doing actions done by X or having experiences that X had, that Y is X. (iii) It is possible to establish beyond reasonable doubt, at least on some occasions, that one of these standards is satisfied without first of all establishing in some other way (by reference to the other) that Y is X.

I think that this use of 'criterion' is different from that given the term by many philosophers in their discussions of outer criteria of inner mental states, or in discussion of so-called factual criteria for the application of evaluative predicates. The basic difference lies in the suggestion here that there is a deductive connection between the satisfaction of the criterion and the conclusion that Y is X. I incline to think, however, that something like the above is what many philosophers have had in mind when they have talked about bodily identity and memory as two criteria of personal identity. They have usually gone on to discuss whether condition (iii) is really satisfiable in the case of memory, and whether, if it is, we could without difficulty envisage a world in which *only* memory was a criterion. I would answer 'Yes' to the first of these questions and 'No' to the second. But before proceeding we must look at other details.

The restriction to two criteria of identity might seem arbitrary and unrealistic. Are there not hosts of reasons for identifying people? There are indeed very many physical characteristics which enable us to recognize our friends, and many more formal tests which can be used in special circumstances to decide who someone is. There are fingerprint tests, blood tests, distinguishing marks, and the like. It is unquestionably somewhat overschematic for philosophers to sum all these together in phrases like 'bodily identity' or 'bodily continuity', but the tests that we use would not in fact tell us what they do tell us if we could not presume that it is a conventional truth that a person is, whatever else we hold him to be, a continuous physical organism undergoing patterns of change appropriate to the type of organism he is. It is a truism of this sort that explains why the tests of identity are not of a kind that rule out change altogether.[1] Circumstances might arise that made us change our concepts so that certain sorts of discontinuities, such as bodily exchanges, were allowed under the concept of a person, but we must postpone consideration of this. We must also put aside the suggestion that bodily identity is not a criterion of personal identity at all because we can find human bodies that do not now belong to persons, viz. corpses and live but grossly impaired organisms. This does not show that where we are, *ex hypothesi*, speaking of a *person* and asking whether he can be identified with some *person* previously known, we cannot decide affirmatively if we know that he has the body that the former person had.

In the case of both our criteria we can use many tests to determine whether a candidate is physically continuous with someone he claims to be, or remembers his actions or experiences. This would make some philosophers inclined to call the facts that serve as such tests themselves criteria for identity in some weaker sense than the one I have used. I have suggested that their serving in this way is due to the fact that they enable us to determine the continuity of the body of the claimant and the person he claims to be, and that there is a deductive connection between this decision and that to call them the same. Among corresponding 'non-physical' facts of great significance (as Quinton's story shows), are similarities of character and skills. These often affect our decision as to who someone is. But only in the case of having X's memories and being X is the connection deductive. I can have my father's character or personality with-

[1] On this see my 'Hume on Personal Identity'.

out being my father; whereas I cannot have his memories, for to do so would be to be my father. Hence similarity of character or of skill (always assuming these can realistically be thought of as non-physical)[1] without memory would be worthless, and they tend to be mere corroborative tests at times when we are unsure whether Y's apparent memories are real ones. In consequence there seems no temptation to suggest that one could give sense to the notion of non-physical continuance by reference to character similarity alone, as there is in the case of memory. Nor is it at all clear what similarity of character without appropriate memories comes to beyond coincidence of personality-traits such as jocularity or solemnity; so any closeness of character that would enter seriously into identity disputes would be of a sort that would entail some appropriate memories.

I am prepared to accept that memory is a criterion of identity in the way in which I have defined this term, but will argue that its being this depends in critical ways upon the existence of the bodily criterion of identity. I draw heavily here upon the contributions of Sydney Shoemaker.[2]

It is tempting to think that accepting the memory-beliefs that others have, and especially accepting their ostensible memories of their own pasts, can only be rationally founded upon observation of the reliability of individual men's memories. If this were true, it would suggest that memory could not be, in my sense,

[1] See B. A. O. Williams, 'Personal Identity and Individuation'.
[2] Sydney Shoemaker, article 'Personal Identity and Memory', and book *Self-Knowledge and Self-Identity*. The quotations in this chapter are from the article.

a criterion, since it would not seem that we could be entitled to say that someone now before us remembers doing X's actions or having X's experiences without either first of all having discovered from his physical features that he is X, or having a great deal of corroboration that the candidate has a trustworthy memory—which would also, in all likelihood, entail independent knowledge of the past life to which he is laying claim. If memory is not a criterion of identity, then certainly the puzzle stories would not exert the temptations they do exert upon us. We can now examine this temptation.

To decide that someone really does remember something is usually to evaluate positively memory-*claims* that he makes. These are normally put in the form of sentences beginning with 'I remember . . .' The cases that are most pertinent to the issue of self-identity are cases where the claims so expressed are claims to remember doing or experiencing actions or events in the past history of the person in question, rather than claims to remember facts. Shoemaker has argued against the view that our reliance upon people's memory-claims in such situations is inductively based. He argues that it is a necessary truth that memory-claims are usually true. I incline to accept his arguments; though for present purposes it is enough for me only to accept them for the sake of the argument, since to reject them would be to reinforce the conclusions which I wish to establish. His arguments are as follows. (i) If someone frequently said with sincerity that he remembered events which did not occur, we would be justified in concluding that he did not know how to use the term 'remember'. (ii) If a child learning the language were to behave in this way with the word 'remember' or its cognates, we would say he had not yet learned how to use it. (iii) If we were translating an unknown language and were inclined to translate certain expressions in it as memory-expressions, our decision whether to do so would have to hinge in part upon the truth or falsity of the statements beginning with those expressions: if they were generally false, we could not translate them in this way.

I incline to think that unless a sceptic is prepared to deny that our language has certain features (that its users are generally successful in communicating by means of it and that it is learned), these arguments do at least refute any generalized scepticism about memory. (I think, incidentally, that parallel arguments could be constructed in connection with other epistemologically important notions like 'see' or 'know'; that it is a logical truth that many of the things people claim to see are there, and many of the things people claim to know are true.) Shoemaker puts the conclusion in the following way:

> . . . inferences of the form 'He claims to remember doing X, so he probably did X' are not simply inductive inferences, for they are warranted by a generalisation that is logically rather than empirically true.

The generalization he refers to is the generalization that 'memory beliefs, and therefore honest memory claims, are generally true'. Let us accept this generalization, not spending time over whether its clear dependence on contingent facts about the learning of language makes it inappropriate to call it a necessary truth. At any rate, it does not seem to be an inductive one. Let us also put aside the question of whether the argument justifies us in saying that memory-claims must be true usually, often, or merely some of the time. What this shows is that it at least can be, and perhaps must often be, in order to accept a man's claims to remember doing something or experiencing something without applying external checks to these claims. Since the truth of such claims entails the identity of the speaker with the person who did or experienced those things, it seems reasonable to conclude that it will often be right to identify people solely on the basis of their memory-claims, without applying other, e.g. physical, tests. And this makes memory a criterion in my sense.

But this last conclusion, if sound, has to be hedged around with qualifications: (*a*) Even though generalized scepticism about memory may be absurd, scepticism about *particular* memory-claims is not. To know that even most memory-claims are correct is not to know which ones these are. It is obvious that the argument at most shows that there may be need of some *reason* for doubt for any doubt to be reasonable; but the lamentable fact of human error is enough to show that it often is. When it is, the truth of the memory-claims before us has to be established, or at least defended. (*b*) Among the wide variety of cases that appropriately generate reasons for doubt are, of course, the cases where we are trying to establish who someone is. (*c*) We can see, further, as Shoemaker has pointed out, that the argument itself requires the existence of tests or checks on memory-claims. For we have to have a use for the distinction between true and false memory-claims; for us to have such a use we must be able to recognize instances of each, and this requires a capacity to make use of some *independent* means of determining whether the man did do or experience what he claims to remember doing or experiencing. It is hard to see what means there could be if physical means of testing this could not be used. (*d*) As Shoemaker further points out, in order to elicit and recognize people's claims to remember, we have to be able to converse with them, and this entails an ability to recognize them at least over short periods of time; so there must be some means or other of doing this other than through the acceptance of the memory-claims they are making.

These last two points can be expanded. For us to know that any memory-claim about a man's own past, which there is reason to doubt, is true, we have to be able (*a*) to recognize him throughout a contemporary period of time, (*b*) to have access to our own, or some third party's, records or recollections of the stretch of past personal history to which he lays claim, and (*c*) to identity the owners of these two with each other on the basis of considerations other than the content of the memory-claims themselves. These are in principle unavailable if the memory-criterion stands alone without the bodily criterion. Hence memory could not be the only standard of personal identity, since if it were it could not, paradoxically, be applied. It is, then, not an *independent* criterion.

The emptiness of the suggestion that memory could be the sole criterion of personal identity is due, in effect, to the incoherence of the view that memories are self-authenticating. But it also has more practical sources. People forget their pasts, or a very great part of them, and we would in daily life be in a paralysing predicament if we had nothing to use to determine who someone was, and no basis for the recognition of our friends, save their memory-claims. The occasions of actual recall of the past, though frequent, are not frequent enough for this. Yet people are at all times physically present at some point in space where observation is possible—or at least not prevented by the absence of a physical body. So physical tests of identity have a constant availability which people's recollections do not. There are two aspects to this, both of which are properly stressed by those who have argued that bodily identity is the more fundamental criterion of the identity of persons. Since bodies are spatio-temporally continuous, it is, first, always possible to try to determine who someone is by scrutinizing his physical characteristics, even though he cannot recall some critical deed or experience in his past; and, second, when he does claim to remember his past his claim can only be true if he was physically present at the episode he seems to recall. So if the bodily tests indicated that this person was not physically present when the deed was done, or the event he claims to have witnessed happened, we would reject his memory-claims.

I have so far treated it as uncontroversial that we can, if need be, apply the bodily criterion of identity without resort to the memory-criterion. There is an apparent objection to this. In applying physical tests, especially in checking on a person's physical presence at past events, it is essential to rely on one's own memory or on that of witnesses. This might seem to show that the bodily criterion of identity is dependent on memory in a way parallel to the memory-criterion's dependence on it. In a way it does show this, but it does not affect the priority of the bodily criterion. For what is shown here is that we are dependent on our memories in not being able to carry through any cognitive procedure whatever without using them. This, however, does not show that when engaged in the cognitive procedure of determining who someone is we cannot, at least in theory, dispense with the memory-claims *of the person himself*, and it is this that we would need to prove to show that there is parity of dependence between the two standards.

These considerations suggest that while both bodily identity and real memory are sufficient conditions of personal identity, the notion that memory would be sufficient if bodily identity were not sufficent also is absurd. Bodily identity is a necessary, as well as a sufficient, condition for the identity of persons. This in turn suggests that the enterprise of attempting to give an intelligible account of the identity of a dis-embodied person in terms of memory alone is doomed to failure.

CHAPTER 6

INCORPOREAL IDENTITY

I HAVE argued that the memory-criterion of identity is only available to us because there is another, viz. bodily identity, and that the memory-criterion only functions because there are physical tests that we can use to determine who someone is. The question before us is whether or not this shows it to be impossible to formulate an intelligible notion of the identity of a disembodied person. It is not yet obvious that we cannot do so if we are willing to accept that we cannot expect to be in a position to *know* whether the conditions of such a person's identity are satisfied at any time.

But the arguments in the previous chapter do not show merely that we need physical tests in order to *know* whether men's memories can establish their identities. They also reveal that without availability of these physical tests there could *be no reason* for the application of the concept of personal identity. And the removal in the doctrine of survival of the availability of the tests entails the removal of the possibility of such a reason in the disembodied case, not merely the removal of our chances of knowing whether this or that test is satisfied.

When discussing post-mortem predication we postulated that a survivor might have, for example, certain visual or auditory imagery, and then asked whether, if he could exercise control over it, this was enough to entitle us, at least in some attenuated sense, to say that he saw, or heard, even though we could never be in a position to know that he had this imagery. If the answer was affirmative, this did not show that either the imagery or the capacity to control it were anything less than essential conditions for the use of the notions of seeing or hearing in our intellectual fantasy. To say that one could admit the coherence of a hypothesis without knowing whether the conditions provided in it actually obtain is not to say that the conditions themselves are not, *in the hypothesis*, essential for the key concepts of that hypothesis to be used. The position is similar with identity and memory. The fact that in a hypothesis of disembodied survival we might not know whether some conditions for self-identity obtained would not itself show (without independent argument) that disembodied identity could not be intelligibly predicted; but this is not to say that the conditions themselves can be dispensed with. The doctrine of disembodiment unfortunately does also dispense with them.

The concept of memory is itself an epistemic one. To say that someone remembers is to say that he has knowledge of a special sort about the past, not merely that he has some present experience or makes some present claim about the past. To say that he remembers doing a certain action, or having a certain experience, is to say that he knows that he did it or experienced it. But he and we cannot know this without understanding what it is for him to have done it or for him to have experienced it. This cannot be articulated in terms of any experience he now has, or any sentence he now utters to us or to himself. For it to be true that he really remembers and does not merely seem to do so (to us or to himself) it must be the case that he, and not another person, did the action or had the experience, and our understanding of this cannot be articulated in terms of any experience he now has, or any sentence he now utters. Memory, as Butler reminded us, presupposes personal identity and cannot serve to define it. What I have referred to as physical tests of identity are physical facts about the present and past of embodied persons which help us to understand and articulate the identity which memory presupposes. This does not mean that any particular test, especially such things as photograph or fingerprint tests, must yield a conclusive result in practice. But it does mean that when we say the memory-criterion is satisfied for an embodied person we imply that there are physical facts which, if known to us, would suffice to establish the identity of the claimant and the original person, for they would establish continuity of the body between them. The fact that, for general epistemological reasons, it must sometimes be in order to dispense with the search for these facts does not mean that this implication is not present when we state that he really does remember. (That one statement implies another does not mean that we cannot have sound reasons for accepting the one without establishing the other first.)

So there are general reasons of principle for rejecting the suggestion that we can render the identity of a disembodied person intelligible, since the subtraction of the body leaves the notion of genuine memory chronically incomplete. Let us now take a closer look at ways in which we might try to articulate disembodied identity, to see how this pessimism is borne out in detail.

I must begin by saying that I can attach no sense to the notion of 'loose' or unowned experiences (or agentless actions). When I feel partially able to grasp the sense of the notion of a sensation that no one has, or an act that no one performs, I immediately reject the notion as flagrantly self-contradictory. If this is not idiosyncratic, it would seem that we can only envisage the psychical remains of persons as belonging to continuing subjects, which we may hope to identify with pre-mortem persons. Prima facie, however, there is also difficulty about the notion of the ownership of experiences in a disembodied state, in view of the fact that we identify the owner of experiences in the embodied state by reference to his physical presence. I have no wish to proceed as though there is no puzzle about understanding reference to a subject that has no body, merely because I also fail to understand how there could be experiences that had no owner at all. On the other hand, I do not wish to base arguments about the coherence of the notion of disembodied existence upon any particular analysis of the present ownership of experiences in the embodied state. So I will concentrate on the *re*-identification of the owner of experiences. Let us ask, then, about the identity of a disembodied person at time T_2 with a disembodied person at time T_1, and the identity of a disembodied person at time T_2 with an embodied person at time T_1.

What makes the owner of experience E_2 at T_2 the same as the owner of experience E_1 at T_1? (Whatever ownership is to be taken to mean here. Once again there is a dilemma: it is natural to put this question in terms of two experiences and what it is that makes them part of the same life-history; but this assumes the intelligibility of independent reference to the experiences without reference to the subjects that have them, which I have to question. On the other hand, in order to talk of them as owned, it is necessary to assume the intelligibility of reference to their owners, which in the present context is doubtful also. I have no wish to minimize the seriousness of this difficulty. On the contrary, I would emphasize it. But it is possible to reveal the defects in the attempt to define disembodied identity without lingering further upon this dilemma, and hardly possible otherwise. I grasp the latter horn of the dilemma to proceed.)

The only available answer seems to be that the owner of E_2 is identical with the owner of E_1 because the owner of E_2 remembers E_1. It is clear, first, that 'remembers' here must mean 'really remembers' not merely 'seems or claims to remember', for our recollections are often faulty. It is also clear, second, that 'remembers' must mean here 'does remember', not just 'can remember'. Attempts to define personal identity in terms of memory (such as that of Locke) have always run into this difficulty. People forget. 'This is the man who drove past the policeman' does not entail 'This man remembers driving past the policeman', even if we assume he noticed doing it at the time. It is useless to counter with the notion of potential recollection and say that it entails 'This man *could* remember driving past the policeman', for in its only harmless interpretation this claim is false. It is not a logical consequence of his having driven past the policeman that *any* practical device would enable him to recall doing it. The only interpretation of 'He could remember' which makes it true that the entailment holds is one in which it means, roughly, '*No one else* could remember', and this notion obviously depends on a prior understanding of his identity with the driver. So in our present case the concept of potential memory of E_1 cannot be used, on pain of circularity. So the only use of 'remember' that is satisfactory here is the one in which it is taken to mean actual, and true recollection of E_1 on the part of the owner of E_2. So the disembodied person having E_2 is the same as the disembodied person who had E_1 if and only if, in addition to having E_2, he remembers (in this strong sense) having E_1.

This runs into two major and connected difficulties. (i) We have to give sense not only to 'the person having E_1' and 'the person having E_2', which we have left aside, but to the complex notion of the person who has E_2 also having a memory (in this case of E_1)—for only an actual recollection will do. If the having of E_2 and the having of this memory are *successive* experiences, this is the very notion we are trying to articulate, and the enterprise already collapses. If they are simultaneous we face the distinct but equally obscure problem of what it is for two contemporary experiences to be experiences of the same person rather than of different persons. This seems to presuppose an understanding of what individuates one person from another, which is absent in the disembodied case. Many contemporaneous experiences occur in our world, and any two of them may belong to the same person and may not, and in the embodied world we usually have no problem in determining which way it is. But in speaking of bodiless persons, there seems as much problem in knowing what is to be understood by two experiences being experienced together by the same subject and not by two distinct subjects as there is in knowing what is to be understood by two experiences being experienced successively by the same subject rather than by two. The temptation is to try to make memory do duty once again and say that two simultaneous experiences are both had by the same subject if and only if they are both remembered together. But the emptiness of this move is readily apparent. If their being remembered together means their being remembered to have occurred together, the circularity is right on the surface. If their being remembered together means their being both remembered by the same person, we merely return to our original problem. And if we tried to avoid these difficulties by making it mean their being remembered in one act of recall, then since one of the two recollected experiences is itself a recollection, we would put a strain upon the notion of recalling two or more experiences simultaneously, for the recollection of the memory would have to be an instance of recalling recalling E_1, not merely recalling *that* one recalled E_1; beside which, it would make it logically impossible for a disembodied person to have two experiences simultaneously without recalling them together.

(ii) The second difficulty is simpler and more basic.

E_1 has to be really remembered, i.e. remembered correctly. This means not merely that someone had E_1 as it is recalled, but that the owner of E_2 is that person. This still presupposes some independent sense for the claim that the owner of E_1 and E_2 are the same. There is nothing new here. But it would be odd if it were expected that there could be. This difficulty is not eased by the suggestion that in weaving our fantasies we can stipulate that there are in fact no erroneous recollections in the disembodied state. This proposal itself makes use of the very notion of identity we are trying to account for. A memory of an experience, even a true one, is not just one more experience, but a manner of knowing one's own past. So we must have some way of making sense already of the claim that E_1 happened to the person owning E_2 and not to another person. For this is *part of the stipulation* that the recollections persons in the next world have are all correct. This stipulation is nothing more than the assertion that the experiences disembodied persons seem to remember having they did in fact have; and we cannot understand this stipulation unless we understand what it excludes, and unless we have some idea what sorts of facts would, if they were known (which they might not be) be sufficient to warrant us to pronounce the seeming memories to be real ones. A parallel difficulty faces the suggestion that we stipulate that only one disembodied person would think he recalled any particular action or experience. Here, too, the understanding of the stipulation presupposes the understanding of the possibility that *not only one* person would think he recalled it, which we cannot have without knowing what it would be for one to think he recalled it and be wrong—or, therefore, right. Memory is essentially a parasitic concept, and needs a body to feed on.

The venerable doctrine of spiritual substance comes to mind here. Historically this notion has served dualistically-minded philosophers as a means of providing continuous ownership for the sequences of thoughts and feelings that make up men's mental lives. The main criticism levelled against it is to be found in Locke's discussion on personal identity, though Locke fails to draw out the full implications of it. Since the concept of substance is not an empirical one, there is no publicly usable set of devices for determining the continued presence of a substance, so its presence cannot serve as a criterion for applying the expression 'the same person' in ordinary life. Locke is reduced to suggesting that the criterion he does argue for (memory) happens by the goodness of God to lead us to ascribe identity on those occasions when the metaphysical substrate does persist, and only on those occasions. It might be suggested that this epistemological difficulty is irrelevant in our present context. But the inutility of the concept of substance is a sign of something deeper. Beyond the wholly empty assurance that it is a metaphysical principle which guarantees continuing identity through time, or the argument that since we know identity persists some such principle must hold in default of others, no content seems available for the doctrine. Its irrelevance to normal occasions for identity-judgments is due to its being merely an alleged identity-guaranteeing condition of which no independent characterization is forthcoming. Failing this, the doctrine amounts to no more than a pious assurance that all is well, deep down. It provides no reason for this assurance.

Thus far I have argued along the following lines. Memory could not be the sole and independent criterion of personal identity, since this would undermine the distinction between true and false memory beliefs about one's past, a distinction which can only exist if there is some further content to the notion of the identity of the rememberer and the owner of the action or experience remembered. Since this further content seems to derive from the possession of a body, or at least to be absent when this possession is excluded, the notion of a persistence through time of a disembodied being, and of its identification with a premortem being, does not seem intelligible.

This argument assigns a priority to physical tests of identity over the memory-criterion. Yet the literature contains puzzle-stories that are designed to tempt us to assign the priorities in the other direction. The suggestion is that when the implications of these puzzle-stories are drawn out, they will show that the physical tests of identity are not as fundamental as I have argued. If this were granted, it might be thought that my argument loses its force, and we might be able to conceive readily enough that a person might retain his identity in separation from the particular body he now has, or even in separation from any. I wish to argue that although the first of these possibilities is intelligible it manages to be intelligible for reasons which rule out the second; that the puzzles are in fact without relevance to the problem of survival.

In arguing this I shall try to take account of the fact that the stories do in fact tempt us to say what their authors wish us to say. They do tempt us to say that the memory-criterion of identity might override physical tests. This fact is very odd if one recalls our earlier account of the relationship between them. We can reinforce this oddity. Even though the memory-criterion requires for its exercise the existence of physical tests of identity, the reverse, as we saw, does not seem true. I do not mean here that one could apply physical tests of identity without making use of men's memories. No epistemological task can be performed without this. To appy tests of a man's identity we need to be able to make use of our own stored knowledge, the testimony of witnesses, the recollection of the known facts about fingerprinting and blood testing, and the rest. What is clearly true, though, is that these tests can be applied to determine who someone is without our *having* to have recourse to the memory-beliefs of the person whose identity we are trying to settle. This apparent independence makes it all the more strange that we should be tempted, as we are, to admit that we can spin tales of our flesh-and-blood world which suggest that physical tests might be negative in their import and yet give place to an identity-judgment based on memory. I will now turn to one example (an inflated version of Locke's) of putative bodily transfer; then to a well-known example of putative reincarnation.

CHAPTER 7

'BODILY TRANSFER'

ONCE upon a time there was a kingdom ruled over by a handsome prince, whose youth had been filled with daring escapades and travels. One morning his servants went to wake him as usual, but a very strange phenomenon met their eyes when they entered. There before them, or so it seemed, was their prince; yet he had a lost and rather frantic expression on his face, and was intermittently staring down at his shoes. His servants wished him good morning, and instead of the usual lofty nod they were treated to a series of entreaties. They were asked to explain where they all were, who they all were, and what all these beautiful clothes and shoes were. He then asked to be taken to the prince, because he wished to explain his presence in the palace, he said; though he was at a loss how to do this. The servants in turn were at a loss how to reply to this request, but one of them bravely told him that he *was* the prince. This he denied, pointing to the portrait of the prince on the wall and saying that *that* was the prince, whom he had often seen pass by in the street. He was the cobbler from the other end of the city, and should really be at work by now. Then the climax came; one of them showed him his face in a mirror. He cried out and protested that he had a different body the night before, and recounted how he had been mending shoes till midnight and had hit his thumb several times because he was sleepy. The servants sent for the palace doctor; but before he could get there there was a great commotion at the palace gate. It seemed that a similar situation had arisen at the cobbler's house, where someone who appeared to be obviously the cobbler had woken up and demanded to be taken away from this dingy house and back to the palace where he belonged. Scoldings from the cobbler's wife had made no difference; he had protested that he did not know who she was, that he must have been kidnapped, and that she should not hector him in the tone she was using. He then forced his way out towards the palace, followed by the protesting woman, and insisting that he was the prince. When he reached the palace the guards refused to let him in, but were discomfited by his apparent recognition of them and his knowledge of the names of the palace servants. They sent for these people, who were still in a baffled state from their encounter with the man in the prince's bedroom. Questioning revealed that the man who looked like the cobbler seemed to recall nothing of the cobbler's late-night shoe-mending, but all sorts of things about the past adventures of the prince, which he insisted were his own doings. He then demanded to be treated as his station required, and told them to put the impostor in his bedroom out of the gates. They found the man in the bedroom quite willing to go, and finally agreed to this solution over the protests of the cobbler's wife, who said that if her husband were going to be kept like royalty, she ought to be, too. Were they right?

I shall take it for granted that since we have never been in a situation quite like the one imagined, a decision as to whether the two men in the story should be regarded as the persons they *claim* to be, rather than the ones they *appear* to be, is indeed one that involves us in a certain degree of innovation; so that an answer to our question is not a mere matter of making explicit a decision we have already made implicitly, but of making a new one. In making it, however, we have to try to stay as close as possible to the conceptual conventions we already follow, if we are to avoid inconsistencies. The difficulty of the puzzle seems to me to lie in the fact that our instincts are indeed as Locke says they are, viz. to accept that this is a case of bodily transfer, yet a careful examination of our current conventions suggests the reverse reading.

For we are only able to use men's memory-beliefs because of the possibility of using physical tests to confirm who people are, and even when we are entitled to accept men's memory-claims without applying these tests, in doing so we commit ourselves to the existence of facts which would independently guarantee a claimant's identity if we knew them. So if we adhere to the conventions that we have, we should unhesitatingly reject claims like those made in our story, where the physical tests are negative consistently. Further, we have seen that in order to elicit and recognize people's memory-claims we have to be able to listen to them over a period of time and therefore be able, by normal physical means, to recognize them throughout that time. And for there to have been a past for our claimants in the story to refer to it must have been possible for others to have observed them and recognize them by normal physical means, throughout a substantial period. For both of these requirements to be met, the normal physical evidence of identity has to be presupposed.

This does not, unfortunately, show that we could not read the puzzle-story the way that someone like Locke would wish. We can, or almost.

Locke could argue as follows. Granted that there has to be a continuing present human body for the speaker of memory-claims (and the bearer of character-traits) to be identified; granted that there has to have been a continuing past body for us to recognize the past history which the present memory-claims are about. Surely these requirements are satisfied in the case of our prince and cobbler? The sets of memory-claims made are in each case made by an identifiable continuing present person; and the past cobbler and prince were readily identifiable in the past and are known to have done and experienced the very things now being described in the past tense. The only oddity is that the body that the cobbler's claims seem to fit is not the one now uttering them; and the body the princely claims fit is not the one now uttering them. We have all the physical adjuncts that are necessary. The fact that the claims are so systematic and consistent makes it thoroughly reasonable to say that there has been bodily transfer.

I think this argument is incontestable. It is possible to say this. I think such cases would have to be exceptional, but I will not argue this here.[1] What it is important to stress is that our story has done nothing

[1] I have argued it in 'Personal Identity'.

to give clear content to the notion of a person going *out of* one body *into* another body, or of a person existing with *no* body. (The latter possibility seems a necessary condition of the first.) For this language carries the implication that what leaves one habitat and enters another is an entity identifiable independently of either body. The argument does nothing, in other words, to warrant Locke's choice of language in describing the case—'Should the soul of a prince . . . enter and inform the body of a cobbler'. Our story gives sense to the notion of two persons exchanging bodies, but none to the notion of these persons existing independently of the bodies which they exchange.

If we accepted the description of our story that involved the prince and the cobbler changing bodies, then we would be committed to the following conceptual innovation: we could henceforth only infer personal identity from bodily identity in cases where there were no systematic memory-claims to suggest that the person now before us did actions and had experiences in the past that were done 'in' another identifiable body. Needless to say, this would be an inconvenient change, and the claims would have to be very systematic indeed. It would amount, of course, to a weakening of the bodily criterion of identity to a position of relative parity with the memory-criterion.

But it is not the only reading of our story. We could also insist on not abandoning the primacy of bodily identity. We could do this in perhaps two ways. One way which suggests itself is that of weakening the memory-criterion by making a major change in the concept of memory, and allowing it to be possible for someone not only to remember actions and experiences in his own past, but also to remember those in the past of another. But this is not as helpful or coherent a suggestion as it looks. We already can remember actions and experiences in the lives of others. We can remember witnessing another doing them or having them, and we can remember *that* he did or had them. All that we cannot do is to remember doing them or remember having them. For this is to remember one's own doing or one's own having of them. To suggest that we could change the sense of 'remember' so that one could remember doing someone else's actions or having someone else's experience is to pass the bounds of possible linguistic legislation, since it is to suggest that one could say something which had the effect of committing us to the possibility of some past action or experience belonging uniquely to two different people, and this is self-contradictory. This can be brought out by expanding our story. Suppose the one who physically appears to be the prince says, 'I remember mending shoes last night', and is then convinced, by reports on his physical characteristics and those of the cobbler, that it was not he who mended the shoes but the cobbler. It would not suffice for him to correct his earlier statement to read 'I remember the cobbler mending the shoes'. This already has a use that would still be needed in the language, viz. the use for claiming knowledge of the cobbler's past actions that comes from having witnessed the cobbler performing them. To give 'remember' a new use to cover the new type of knowledge of another's past would be to make it impossible to distinguish this new type from the ordinary recollections of a witness.

There is a simpler and more viable way in which we

might retain intact both our present standards of identity and yet adjust to these startling events. We might invent a new word to cover cases of what seem to be memories (because of their accuracy, their presentation in the first person singular past tense, etc.), but cannot *be* memories (because they fit the wrong body). I suggest the concept of retrocognition. We could say that the cobbler and prince retrocognize one another's pasts. Such a strange phenomenon would naturally go with the adoption of one another's characters—at least if, when I began to retrocognize my neighbour's past, I proceeded to forget my own.

This way of preserving present practice involves no change in the use of current concepts, only the introduction of a new one. Not, of course, a very clear one, but perhaps a usable one. My present point is that such an alternative does exist and can deal with our case of putative bodily transfer as easily as the hypothesis of *actual* bodily transfer. This does, however, with the restrictions imposed, remain one possible and reasonable reading of our story.[1] Furthermore, we feel, I think, an instinctive *preference* for it, even though there seem to be no good reasons for such a preference. There are, I think, two reasons for such a preference, both philosophically disreputable.

The first derives from imagining oneself one of the protagonists in the story. Surely if we do this we can see that anyone possessed of all these memories would *know* quite clearly who he was? Surely he would know that he had a new body (or rather, another)? How could even the most numerous collection of third parties tell him he was wrong?

[1] And of A. M. Quinton's.

We are mistaken if we yield to this.

A criterion of identity has to be part of a publicly-usable set of conceptual devices. (There is no sense to the suggestion that someone is one person to himself and another to others, unless this means that he is concealing his identity from them by a disguise or something equally uninteresting.) Now what makes memory a criterion of identity is the fact that people make their memories public property by making memory-claims, by *saying* that they remember things. And what makes these claims correct, what shows that people are remembering and not imagining is the fact that these claims can be tested publicly. Someone who says he remembers is not making an introspective report, but a public knowledge-claim, which is corrigible in the same way that claims to see or hear are. But, of course, only the person himself has the experience (the image, or whatever) which most people say they have when they remember, and which serves presumably as the *occasion* for the claim. This is important as a fact of psychology, but not with regard to the status of memory-claims themselves. This is the general sort of context in which we learn to *make* memory-claims. But when someone, as in our story, has the usual sort of memory-experience he is disposed to use the normal memory-language, and say, e.g., 'I remember mending the shoes.' To say that he must be right because only he has the appropriate present *experiences* is to overlook that the decisions and investigations of others, as much as his own experiences, are necessary before he can be said to be entitled to claim to *remember*.

It is familiar enough for you or I to think we remember something and find out that we are mistaken—after which we say that we didn't really remember, but only thought that we did. But any experience we had is still part of our mental history just as much as it was when we took it as a memory. So it is easy enough to imagine being one of the people in the story and thinking that one remembered. This does not, without further decision, justify our saying that this amounts to *accepting* their memory-claims, which there is reason not to do. But imagining apparent memories is no different from imagining real ones, since the inner experiences would be the same; hence the ease with which it is taken for granted that one would be doing the second rather than the first.

The second source of our instinctive preference for saying that our heroes have changed bodies rather than experienced some radical upheaval in their memories is more familiar. It is the deep commitment of most of us in our interpretative thinking to psychophysical dualism. We seem to believe in an independently identifiable purely psychical entity which inhabits the body and can leave it and go to another. An examination of our story and our identification practices shows that such a concept is not coherent and not borne out by the imaginary events. It is not coherent because the only criterion of identity for such an entity would be memory, which we have shown cannot operate as a criterion alone; it is not borne out by the events because to recognize that they have occurred in the way stated is to make use of bodily evidence. Yet the dualistic thesis, bolstered by the use of inappropriate mental pictures, determines our choice in reading the events described.

Of course, since what we would say in actual cases would be determined by such prejudices as this one, no doubt our instinctive preference, philosophically disreputable or not, would determine the common usages which such cases would generate. But this would merely show that the dualistic model was influential, not that it was coherent.

To sum up. We can say that the cobbler and the prince have changed bodies. We can say this because we are able to imagine identifying the pre-change persons through time by reference to the bodies which they had, and to imagine identifying the post-change persons through time by reference to the bodies which they have. But saying this is merely to admit that two people could, at the cost of some conceptual change, be said to *exchange* bodies. It is not to say that they can meaningfully be said to exist independently of the bodies which they exchange. It gives no sense to the conception of a person going *out of* one body *into* another. Further, although we can say they have exchanged bodies, we do not have to do so. We can change our conventions in another way, by inventing the new concept of retrocognition. The only thing that would come near to making the bodily transfer story a *mandatory* reading of the tale of the cobbler and the prince would be our having an independently intelligible notion of that which could be alleged to leave one body and go into the other, and our being able to trace this progress. We may disregard the second of these conditions, for the first is not satisfied. The notion we need is the very one we have been looking for, and the story does not provide it. On the contrary, the story will only serve the purposes that tales of its type are invented to serve in the literature of personal identity if we assume quite incorrectly that we have it already.

CHAPTER 8

'REINCARNATION'

RUTH SIMMONS under hypnosis made elaborate and striking memory-claims that (let us say) 'fitted' the known past of Bridey Murphy. Hypnosis was needed to elicit these memory-claims; they were made in an Irish brogue; and the period they fitted was more than a century before Ruth Simmons's birth. Can one say that Ruth is the reincarnation of Bridey?[1]

As far as I can see one can; but the very facts which enable one to do this also, when understood, reduce the motive for doing it. For we have before us one ostensibly persisting and identical person, embodied; we have records of another in the past; we have no evidence of another body to which Ruth's personality 'goes' during the hypnotic trances. It would seem that one source of temptation to say Bridey has reappeared in Ruth is an extensive 'takeover' of Ruth's personality. (Failing this, we are tempted to speak instead of alternating personalities.) But another source of the temptation is the notion that Bridey has somehow continued to exist in between, disembodied, and has entered into Ruth's body. This, however, is an inco-

[1] See the works cited by Bernstein and Ducasse.

herent notion. The notion that Ruth is Bridey has to mean that these are the two successive bodies of the same person, *without there being* a purely psychical intermediate state. For this is the only source of the notion of a person going *out of* and *into* bodies. Without this notion, however, the description in terms of some remarkable faculty of retrocognitive clairvoyance is a less inconvenient and equally viable alternative: always assuming that we have here a case that requires paranormal explanation at all.

So we can say that Ruth is Bridey. Once again, of course, the possibility of our making such an identity-judgment depends on our having two independently traceable life-stories to combine. To say that Ruth is Bridey is not to say that Ruth-Bridey continues dis-embodied in between, and it gives that suggestion no sense of its own. One of the necessary conditions of the identification being mandatory rather than, as at present, optional, is that this suggestion *should* have sense given to it independently. (Another condition is that we should have evidence of this also.) Such independent sense is once again what we have been seeking, and the tale of Ruth and Bridey does not give it to us.

The alternative to identifying Ruth with Bridey is to postulate some sort of paranormal knowledge in Ruth. But that the identification is even an option for us is a result of the fact that we can make it without having to postulate an intermediate disembodied soul. To the question 'What has to exist between one in-carnation and another?' the answer may be 'Nothing'. This answer has to be possible for the doctrine of re-incarnation to be possible. Yet only if the intermediate state could be given an intelligible description could any set of circumstances *require* the doctrine. We fortunately do not need to explore the question of whether the nothingness that falls between Bridey and Ruth implies that the person who is both Ruth and Bridey has gone out of existence in between.[1]

[1] See *Analysis* Competition No. 11, 1957.

CHAPTER 9

RESURRECTION

LET us construct a predictable set of circumstances that seem to fit the concept of the resurrection of men. At some (unspecified) future date, a large number of persons will appear, in bodies like (or somewhat like) our own here and now. Each one will claim to be some person long since dead, will have putative memories that 'fit' his claim to be that person, and will physically resemble that person. It is clear that there is no difficulty about conceiving the sort of existence such people would have; in particular, since they would have human bodies, there is no difficulty at all about their being persisting, re-identifiable individuals *in this future state*. The problem is whether or not they are identifiable with us, the pre-mortem beings who died. It seems to me that there is no compelling reason for saying that they cannot be; nor is there any compelling reason for saying that they have to be. And this has odd consequences.

Let us elaborate the hypothesis. Let us add the stipulation that the number of resurrectees be the same as, or no greater than, the number of deceaseds; let us also add that each one at least begins, before philosophical doubts are raised, by being in no doubt

about who he claims to be, or whose past he makes
first-person memory-claims about; and that no one
claims to be a past person whom he does not resemble
and whose past he is not able to inform us of (in the
first person) with a reasonably high degree of accuracy.
Let us also assume that there are some persons who
have lived through the period during which the sudden
collective (re)appearance has taken place, and can
confirm the above details by diligent research. And let
us suppose ourselves to be among that select number.
Must we say that these are our former friends? While
saying so would indeed be arbitrary if the above conditions were not wholly fulfilled; would it not be the
only reasonable course if they were?

It certainly would, I think, be *a* reasonable course.
But not, puzzlingly, the only reasonable one. If it is
reasonable, as I argued previously, to say that the
cobbler and the prince had indeed changed bodies, even
though we could not say that either of them existed
even momentarily in a non-bodily state; if it is reasonable to say that Bridey has reappeared 'as' Ruth, even
though there be no suggestion that Bridey has endured
between in a non-bodily form; then it is also reasonable
to say that each claimant is the post-mortem phase of
the pre-mortem person he represents himself to be.
(Remember that he can so represent himself with re-
gret and guilt as well as with pleasure.) For one can in
effect regard persons as what might be called gap-
inclusive entities, who disappear into nothing and re-
appear, full-bodiedly, at the resurrection. And their
memory-claims are made by continuous, observable,
flesh-and-blood persons, and are claims *about* continuous, observable, flesh-and-blood persons, and are there-

fore as eligible for acceptance, it seems, as those of the
cobbler and prince: more so, in fact, for they are about
persons who had bodies which are like the bodies uttering them, not radically unlike. And the moral pressure
one would expect to be exerted by what all statistics
suggest would be a very large number of persons, would
add weight to the claim that they should be regarded as
whoever they regard themselves as being.

But just as the parallel decisions in the case of the
bodily transfer story and the reincarnation story are
not necessary, so here, too, the decision, though probably more likely, is still a decision and does not have to
be made one way. For one can also say that what is
predicted is the future appearance of a large number of
persons, each of whom resembles someone dead, and
has unique retro-cognitive access to the past of that
person. (It is worth stressing also that a decision to describe the situation in this way might become as
acceptable a form of speech for describing the remi-
niscences of the resurrectees as the other, and therefore be adopted *by them* as time went on.) And it might
be argued that the existence of the time-gap between
the deaths and the resurrections supplied the reason
for preferring this description.

How is one to decide this issue? Certainly the time-
gap does not necessitate a refusal to identify in this
case, any more than it does in the case of Bridey
Murphy. There is no need for persons to be regarded as
necessarily continuous entities; they might exist like
television serials do, in instalments. But consider the
following problem. It is possible for Smith now to
predict that someone will exist at some future resurrection date just like himself. It is possible for Smith to

imagine that person having memory-like experiences which prompt him to make accurate memory-claims which fit actual previous events in Smith's life. This person is imagined as doing these things at some time after Smith's death. But it is possible for Smith to say that that person is not going to be he, Smith, but someone very like him. If he says this he will say that it would be unfair for that future person to be punished for anything that he, Smith, has done, however willing he is to accept the punishments. And as long as Smith is able to make his predictions in these terms, he can be quite serene and indifferent about those punishments, because, however unfair they are, they will not be meted out *to him*. The fact that there will be someone who thinks he is remembering doing Smith's deeds and therefore accepts the blame for them does not prove that that person will be Smith and therefore does not prove that Smith need care. The critical step for Smith is that of predicting *his own* future resurrected existence.

Now in life we would reject such arguments. Even when people have forgotten doing evil things, we are inclined to hold them responsible; and if they do have memories of them they are so much the more guilty. Even if they fell into a lengthy coma and emerged different in character after it, we would still say that they were the ones who had done the deeds, however much they would now avoid such behaviour. So each of us could go into a coma knowing that when he came out of it he would have to carry the burden of his past. But this is all because there is another way of establishing identity besides the claims of the person himself: there are bodily facts which establish who it is.

The absence of those facts, though perhaps (from our stories) not a fatal barrier to identification on memory-claims alone, certainly renders it optional. With the gap between the death of the one body and the appearance of the resurrection-body all necessity for saying Smith's successor is Smith disappears, however possible it is. And it does not seem that Smith *need* concern himself with being his own successor unless that successor *has* to be identified with Smith. And without the continuity of the body, the identification does not *have* to be performed. The critical difference between a person's looking forward to his own resurrected future and his predicting the future existence of a being like himself seems to depend on a decision which can, in default of bodily continuance, be taken equally well one way or the other.

Two points suggest themselves. One is that the body is, after resurrection, the same one that existed before, not merely a similar one. Let us put aside the question of its possible transformation, and the sticky questions about whether it is the body as it was just before death or as it was in its prime. The fact of the gap means that the decision to say it is the same body will depend on a prior decision to say it is the same person, not the reverse. Secondly it might be suggested that we can 'fill' the gap by having the person imagined as continuing to be between death and resurrection. If this were possible, there would be no problem of identification. But the only possible way in which this can be envisaged is in the form of a disembodied psychical entity. Since this is incoherent, the escape-route it seems to offer is closed. Yet again there seems little doubt that the bland acceptance of the intelligibility of this doctrine of survival has depended in practice upon the assumption of such bodiless continuance.

Finally, it might be suggested that what Smith can correctly be said to be predicting in this case depends simply and solely upon whatever the collective decision is. But this is very baffling. Do we tell Smith now what to expect on the basis of what we think men faced with that situation *then* would say? Do we tell him on the basis of what we now, imagining that future situation, would regard it as wisest to say? Or do we take our cue from the fact that there are many who say they expect the resurrection and are therefore presumably committed ahead of time to a particular interpretation? No one answer seems quite satisfactory here. The last one runs into the problem that those who are committed to the doctrine of resurrection seem also to believe in the intermediate psychic state, which is demonstrably absurd; yet without this belief it is hard to see that their description of what to expect is the only possible one, and if it is not, their prediction can be questioned not only on the ground that perhaps these future beings will not materialize, but also on the grounds we have been considering above. We should not put too much weight on the fact that those who believe in this future set of events would all put one interpretation on them. But if we look back at the first two alternatives, it seems possible for us now to consider that those who *then* interpret these events in a given way may be wrong, and overly swayed by appearances. And if this is even possible, we presumably have to advise Smith now on the basis of our own present decision on how to interpret the hypothetical future event. And again a matter of great cosmic moment seems to hinge on a linguistic decision.

In sum therefore, although our stories seem to suggest that a doctrine of resurrection is logically viable in a way in which a doctrine of disembodied survival is not, there seems no way of constructing it that ensures that it is the only possible reading of the predictions. Only by smuggling in an impossible doctrine of intermediate bodiless existence could this be provided. Lacking this, we are in the same position as in the other puzzle case, of having a choice of possible descriptions —with the difference that the choice matters deeply, though the grounds seem ineluctably incomplete.

In introducing the doctrine of bodily resurrection at the outset, I indicated that I would assume it to be held in a form which claimed the resurrection body and the pre-mortem body to be identical. We have just seen that this cannot be stated in the doctrine without presupposing that the owner of the earlier body and the owner of the later body are the same person. Otherwise the gap in time between the dissolution of the earlier and the appearance of the later body make it quite as easy to say they are merely two similar bodies. It is, however, possible to present the doctrine of resurrection in more than one version. A version which is not tied to the numerical identity of the pre-mortem and post-mortem bodies is outlined by John Hick in Chapter 8 of his book, *Faith and Knowledge*, where he tries to show that we can intelligibly look for post-mortem verification of Christian religious claims.

He gives three pictures, in order. First, a man disappears from a learned gathering in England, and at the same moment a replica of him appears in Australia, complete with all 'memories' and character-traits. In this situation, he urges, we would have no reasonable alternative but to identify them. The second picture is the same as the first except that the disappearance is replaced by a sudden death. Here, he urges, the factors inclining us to say the two persons are identical would outweigh those inclining us to say the opposite. The third picture is the same as the second, except that the replica-person appears not in Australia but in another space altogether, in the resurrection world. The first two pictures are intended to prepare us to admit the logical possibility of the third. This version of a resurrection story might seem to avoid some of the difficulty of our earlier one, which may owe too much to pictures of Doomsday. I think I have repeated here enough of the details of Hick's version to enable an evaluation of it to be made.

His purpose is in the first instance to claim that each picture is intelligible and does not transgress the bounds of logical possibility. This can be conceded, though here I have some difficulty, as before, in attaching sense to the claim that there could be another space not in Space. He wishes also to claim that the identification of the former and the later persons in each of the three pictures is not absurd. This I would also not wish to contest. The difficulty is rather that the identification, though indeed not absurd, is a *decision* and cannot, except perhaps in the case of the first picture, be represented as a discovery. In the first picture it is tempting to think we have a case of a man travelling in a flash for an enormous distance, and we would probably not hesitate long especially if there were a (short) lapse of time between the appearance and the disappearance—and if there were not, we might feel disposed on reflection to abandon the insistence that all human bodies are spatially as well as temporally continuous. In the second picture, however, and even more in the third, identification is *interpretation*, however reasonable. In our first resurrection story we could *say* that the resurrectees had bodies identical with those had by their pre-mortem counterparts. But with the corpse on our hands in the second picture we cannot say this. And with the third picture (which we might call instantaneous putative resurrection instead of delayed putative resurrection) we cannot identify the bodies either, unless the first one has been destroyed. In situations like these it is a matter of decision whether to say that physical tests of identity reveal personal identity or very close similarity. We can, reasonably, decide for identity, but we do not have to. And this seems to leave the description of the future life in a state of chronic ambiguity. One could only *tell* an imaginary objector that his scepticism was mistaken, since it is hard to give sense to the apparently stronger move of informing him that he would discover that he personally would appear as one of the inhabitants of the resurrection world. In order to have grounds for telling him that he cannot reasonably decide his way one would once again need, at least, the ability to use the independently intelligible notion of bodiless personality. And the pictures seem designed to make no use of it.

Perhaps it is possible to present a doctrine of instantaneous resurrection in the form that requires the resurrection body to appear only when the pre-mortem body finally ceases to linger. This complication would be without interest, for in the large number of cases where it lingers for a substantial time we would once again incorporate a time-gap into our story, and again identification would only be mandatory if we added something carrying the identity of the person, which left the pre-mortem body when it died and is to enter the other subsequently. Given the unintelligibility of this, our earlier worry returns. While it seems altogether reasonable, and is certainly logically possible, to *call* the resurrectee the pre-mortem person, and to expect to *treat* him as the pre-mortem person, is this quite enough, when it is not mandatory to do these things (when its being that person does not follow from the data of our stories) to warrant each one of us expecting *himself to be* one of these post-mortem beings in the future?

CHAPTER 10

A HERETICAL POSTSCRIPT

THE answer I have offered to the problem of the intelligibility of the doctrine of survival is not a tidy one, but a tidy answer is not to be expected. I have argued that the doctrine of disembodied survival founders because no intelligible account seems possible in it of the persistence of a disembodied person through time. This is not because the doctrine postulates the future existence of beings about whom the requisite facts could not be known, but because it removes the possibility of the existence of such facts altogether, and requires us to try to make the self-identity of spirits intelligible by reference to memory alone, which is self-defeating. On the other hand, arguments against the intelligibility of disembodied existence which depend on the claim that predicates such as those of perception or agency cannot in principle be applied to non-physical beings seem to me inadequate. The doctrine of disembodied survival is not helped by concentration on the puzzle-stories of the literature of personal identity, for these at most provide an option to speak of this identity transcending the bounds of one particular human body, not of any human body. The doctrine of resurrection is, however, an intelligible one. Its difficulty is rather that, like the hypothesis of bodily transfer and reincarnation, it seems at best an optional reading of the kinds of circumstance that its proponents envisage—or, what comes to the same thing, when resurrection is predicted it is always open to a critic to deny that what is predicted has to be accorded that title. We would only have to accord the title if some intermediate disembodied state were added to the story, and it cannot be.

Such a result cannot be compressed to a simple affirmative or negative. In particular, a simple negative verdict would be out of place for another reason. There are many other possible versions of a belief in survival, which are no doubt less appealing because of their air of tasteless fantasy, but which may be free of the difficulties ours have encountered. A doctrine of astral or ectoplasmic bodies in which departed persons can view our world and occasionally interfere with it is held by some, and if we held to it we might be able to use it to deal with the more intractable phenomena of psychical research. For some, the astral body might be in some way fused in life without earthly body and then separated from it at death, or it might be the body to which the pre-mortem person's identity is transferred in the way in which we might have said our cobbler's identity is transferred to the body of the prince. At least this thesis would evade the radical difficulties of Chapters 5 and 6 while enabling us to make use of the mildly positive results of Chapters 2 and 3: for the astral body need not have all the organs we use for perception or agency, yet might be describable in a way which is intelligible, sufficient to give tolerable imaginative grounds for the ascription of identity through time, and immune to very rapid empirical refutation. Another way of generating a survival doctrine which would, *prima facie*, have some chance of an explanatory use, would be to opt for a thesis of instantaneous resurrection in another space, plus the claim that from that space the resurrectee might clairvoyantly perceive, or even from 'a distance' act in, our world. For the only world from which I claimed to demonstrate that it is logically impossible for this one to be seen is a Next World that is not spatial at all. Temporary bodily transfer from the resurrection world into the body of a medium in this one might not be logically impossible either, for this would not be the same as the hypothesis I toyed with in Chapter 3 of the temporary occupation of her body by a disembodied person; this is indeed ruled out of court by our subsequent difficulties about identity.

I do not recommend these fantasies, or suggest that they cannot be made to yield logical difficulties. Nor do I imagine any philosophers would find them attractive. Christians are likely to find them repellent, which is no doubt why they have shown little more interest in Psychical Research than sceptics have shown. I point out merely that I do not think my earlier arguments rule them out as logically possible options, though I cannot imagine any circumstances which would *require* them. We must always bear in mind the philosophical (and religious) truism that reality may not conform to our theoretical or aesthetic tastes.

As a postscript I shall comment briefly on an even vaster question. I have alluded to the key role which belief in survival plays in the Christian religious tra-

dition. Our discussion of disembodied personality suggests a simple negative argument against a key element in that tradition. In it God is alleged to be
personal, and to be incorporeal. If there are insuperable
difficulties in the concept of a disembodied human person, do they not make it impossible to hold there is a
divine incorporeal person?

God is held to be an incorporeal personal being who
loves his creatures and acts in his creation. If we
address ourselves a little to the much-discussed question of how far such a claim can be understood, it is
apparent very quickly that any theological ban, however natural, on speculation regarding the mind of
God, is not totally enforceable. The only way to try to
avoid such speculation altogether is to try to give
content to a claim like the claim that God loves us by
means of something like a dispositional analysis: to
say that God's loving us, by analogy perhaps with our
inferior love for one another, manifests itself in certain
kinds of *action*. Our problem then is to make the notion of a divine action intelligible. What is the difference between saying of some natural event (or even
some event in human history) that it is also an act of
God? One cannot, as some reductionist analyses of
religious discourse suggest, explain this difference
merely by saying that events like it form a discernible
pattern which has particular human significance, tend-
ing for example to human self-fulfilment or moral edu-
cation. For such an analysis will not serve to distinguish the claim that these events are acts of God from
the mere claim that the world is constantly improving,
or that history is leading towards greater human self-
understanding, or some other platitude of secular

religiosity. The case is no better if we adopt some meta-physical thesis to the effect that the events form a pattern which enable us to ascribe to the world itself some analogue of human purpose, for this, if intelligible at all, merely suggests a form of pantheism. The concept of divine action in the world forces one back on to the reference to the divine individual agent who has the love and performs the actions. If this is accepted, another result follows. For an omnipotent being all actions are basic actions. We cannot consistently say of him that there is something he has to do in order to perform any action that he wishes to perform. But he has no body, and no limbs to move; so the basic actions that he performs do not, as opposed to *our* basic actions, involve any bodily movement. The only movements they embody are those that compose the natural events we are calling his acts. But then, what, again, is added to the account of those events by saying God does them? We cannot answer this by postulating any of the magical willing or formula-reciting that we speculated about in discussing creaturely agency, for this would be inconsistent with the claim that the actions are basic. On the other hand, logic requires that even though an omnipotent being cannot have to go through any process of agency to effect his choices, there must be something in him which gives content to the claim that they are things he has done. So not only can God choose that events happen, but it is logically necessary for the claim that they are his actions to have content that he should *choose*, and have wishes and intentions and thoughts. To some extent at least, the concept of divine agency requires us to postulate a divine mental life to give content to the belief that God acts.

How are we to do this? Total agnosticism about the character of the divine mental life leaves us without the content we need. So also, I believe (though I cannot argue this here), does the claim that God chooses and wishes *timelessly*. If we do not choose these ways of evading the difficulty, we are faced again with the problem that concerned us in Chapters 5 and 6 viz. that of the identity of an incorporeal being through time. This is close to, though not synonymous with, the problem of the identification of the object of theistic worship.[1] If God is incorporeal, how can his worshippers identify him to refer to or, in particular, to address, if one assumes an unwillingness to identify him with the ancillary objects such as altars that are present when some acts of worship are performed? For he cannot exist at one place rather than another. The only possible answer, I think, is to take a hint from this last consideration and recognize that the notion of identification used in this last objection has built into it the concept of distinguishing one object of reference or address *from others*. Clearly no incorporeal being can be so distinguished, not just because he cannot be seen or *picked out*, but because in the absence of any body we cannot give content to the individuation of one such being from another, just as we cannot give content to the notion of some mental act being performed by the same incorporeal being who performed a previous one, rather than by another. But perhaps this only shows that it is incoherent (as indeed it is) to hold there could be a *plurality* of incorporeal beings. It might be possible to hold not that there cannot be any, but that there must either be none, or only one.

[1] See Coburn's essay 'The Hiddenness of God'.

BIBLIOGRAPHY

BERNSTEIN, Morey: *The Search for Bridey Murphy*, Doubleday, New York, 1956.

BRAND, Myles: 'Danto on Basic Actions', *Noûs*, Vol. II, 1968.

BUTLER, Joseph: 'Of Personal Identity', appended to *The Analogy of Religion*, Dent, Everyman edition, 1906, pp. 257–63.

COBURN, Robert C.: 'The Hiddenness of God and Some Barmecidal God Surrogates', *Journal of Philosophy*, Vol. LVII, 1960.

CULLMANN, Oscar: *Immortality of the Soul or Resurrection of the Dead?* Epworth, London, 1958.

DANTO, Arthur: 'What we can do', *Journal of Philosophy*, Vol. LX, 1963.

———: 'Basic Actions', *American Philosophical Quarterly*, Vol. 2, 1965.

———: 'Freedom and Forbearance' in *Freedom and Determinism*, ed. Keith Lehrer, Random House, New York, 1966.

DUCASSE, C. J.: *The Belief in a Life After Death*, Charles C. Thomas, Springfield, Ill., 1961.

FLEW, Antony: 'Locke and the Problem of Personal Identity', *Philosophy*, Vol. 26, 1951.

———: 'Immortality', *Encyclopedia of Philosophy*, ed. Paul Edwards, Macmillan, New York, 1967, Vol. 4.

——: *A New Approach to Psychical Research*, Watts, London, 1953.

——: *Body, Mind, and Death* (ed.), Macmillan, New York, 1964.

——: 'Theology and Falsification' in Flew and MacIntyre (eds.). *New Essays in Philosophical Theology*, S.C.M., London, 1955.

HICK, John: 'Theology and Verification', *Theology Today*, 1960.

——: *Faith and Knowledge*, Cornell, Ithaca, 2nd edition 1966.

MACINTYRE, A. C.: 'A Note on Immortality', *Mind*, Vol. LXIV, 1955.

MALCOLM, Norman: *Dreaming*, Routledge and Kegan Paul, London, 1959.

MUNSAT, Stanley: *The Concept of Memory*, Random House, New York, 1967.

PENELHUM, Terence: 'Hume on Personal Identity', *Philosophical Review*, Vol. LXIV, 1955.

——: 'Personal Identity', *Encyclopedia of Philosophy*, ed. Paul Edwards, Macmillan, New York, 1967, Vol. 6.

——: 'Personal Identity, Memory and Survival', *Journal of Philosophy*, Vol. LVI, 1959.

——: 'Reply to Professor Cauchy', *Proceedings of the Seventh Inter-American Congress of Philosophy*, Les Presses de l'Université Laval, Québec, 1967; symposium 'La notion d'âme, le moi, et l'identité personelle'.

PRICE, H. H.: 'Survival and the Idea of "Another World",' *Proceedings of the Society for Psychical Research*, Vol. 50, 1952, reprinted in J. R. Smythies (ed.), *Brain and Mind*, Routledge and Kegan Paul, London, 1965.

——: 'What Kind of Next World?' in Arnold Toynbee *et*

al., *Man's Concern With Death*, Hodder and Stoughton, London, 1968.

QUINTON, A. M.: 'The Soul', *Journal of Philosophy*, Vol. LIX, 1962.

RYLE, Gilbert: *The Concept of Mind*, Hutchinson, London, 1949.

SHOEMAKER, Sydney: 'Personal Identity and Memory', *Journal of Philosophy*, Vol. LVI, 1959.

————: *Self-Knowledge and Self-Identity*, Cornell, Ithaca, 1963.

STRAWSON, P. F.: *Individuals*, Methuen, London, 1959.

WILLIAMS, B. A. O.: 'Personal Identity and Individuation', *Proceedings of the Aristotelian Society*, Vol. LVII, 1956–7.

WOLFSON, H. A.: 'Immortality and Resurrection in the Philosophy of the Church Fathers', in *Religious Philosophy*, Harvard, 1961.

INDEX